Deptford Show Ground

The last permanent fairground in London

ANGELA CATHERINE CAIN

Grosvenor House
Publishing Limited

The right of Angela Catherine Cain to be identified as the author of this
work has been asserted in accordance with Section 78
of the Copyright, Designs and Patents Act 1988

The book cover is copyright to Angela Catherine Cain

This book is published by
Grosvenor House Publishing Ltd
Link House
140 The Broadway, Tolworth, Surrey, KT6 7HT.
www.grosvenorhousepublishing.co.uk

A CIP record for this book
is available from the British Library

ISBN 978-1-80381-303-5

Dedication

This book is dedicated to the memory of the hard-working community of showmen who lived and thrived on the Deptford Show Ground and to their descendants and to the people of Deptford who enjoyed it so much.[1]

Preface

The Deptford Show Ground played a big part in my childhood, and I was very sad when it was sold when I was just 13 in 1961. I loved to visit the Show Ground and my aunt's travelling fair when it came to Blackheath each bank holiday. My mother and grandmother enjoyed sharing family stories so I absorbed its history without realising it. My family had been associated with the Show Ground since 1890 when my great grandfather, then a 'hawker and traveller', went on to buy it and make his fortune. When my cousins showed me their grandmother Daisy's album about growing up on the Show Ground in the early 1900s, I realised what a special story this was and set about researching it further. As I have been writing it, I have been thinking about how much enjoyment it would have given to local people in an age before television and radio; how it shaped our family history; and how fairground history mirrors changes in wider society. And I thought about the children who now go to school on the site of what was once a fairground and how they would enjoy learning about lion tamers, acrobats, big rides, travelling cinemas, boxing booths and much more. I hope you will enjoy reading it as much as I have enjoyed writing it.

Angela Catherine Cain

Contents   **Page**

Chapter One

Introduction and synopsis

"Tell us the showman's tale, you say. And why not? The very thought of it brings back to my ears the jingle of bells. The dim figures before me turn into a thousand shapes and fancies. Tell you the showman's tale? Ay, that I will. Once more I hear the blare of music and the sound of drums. I catch the laughter of merry children.

Walk up! Walk up! Walk up!"

by Kenneth Grahame[2]

Aerial view of the Deptford Show Ground in the 1930s; *see the fairground house and warehouse in the background and rides and stalls in the middle ground*

Deptford Show Ground was a thriving fairground on Deptford High Street, corner of Giffin Street, from the late nineteenth century to 1961 when it closed its doors for the last time. Charles Cain[3] is recorded as living and working on the "Exhibition Ground" (its name in the early days) from 1891 where he was registered on the Census as a 'hawker and traveller'.

The Show Ground lease was then owned by the Weatherhead family. By 1912 Charles Cain was so successful from his business supplying prizes to fairs that he was able to buy the lease and expanded the Show Ground into both a thriving all-year-round fairground and also a business hub that supplied fairground prizes or 'swag' to fairs across Southern England. *See Chapters 2 and 3.*

Accounts show the Show Ground as a very lively place before and during the First World War and through to the Second World War. In the early days, it was at the forefront of fairground innovation with circus acts, menageries ('wild beast' shows), early cinema (Bioscopes and Cinematographs), music hall and boxing booths, as well as a variety of 'joints' or side shows. *See Chapters 2 and 3.*

A number of well-known showmen families travelled from fair to fair in the summer and spent the winter at the Show Ground, into the 1950s, contributing their rides and stalls to the vibrant atmosphere.

Crowds outside the Show Ground in Deptford High Street in 1911.
©Heritage Images/Getty Images

There was a strong link with the famous annual Mitcham Fair and the special key to open that fair was kept at the Deptford Show Ground and collected by the new mayor each year. *See Chapters 2 and 5.*

The site of the Show Ground was compulsorily purchased in 1961 by the Metropolitan Council of Deptford as part of its regeneration plans for Deptford; it was then used as a car park and the Show Ground buildings were used mainly for storage. The 3-acre site was finally put to good use in 2011 when Tidemill Academy (formerly Tidemill School) was built on the site and also Deptford Lounge, a state-of-the-art library and community hub. Wavelengths Leisure Centre was built on adjacent land – a former stone yard – also previously owned by the Cain family. *See Chapter 2.*

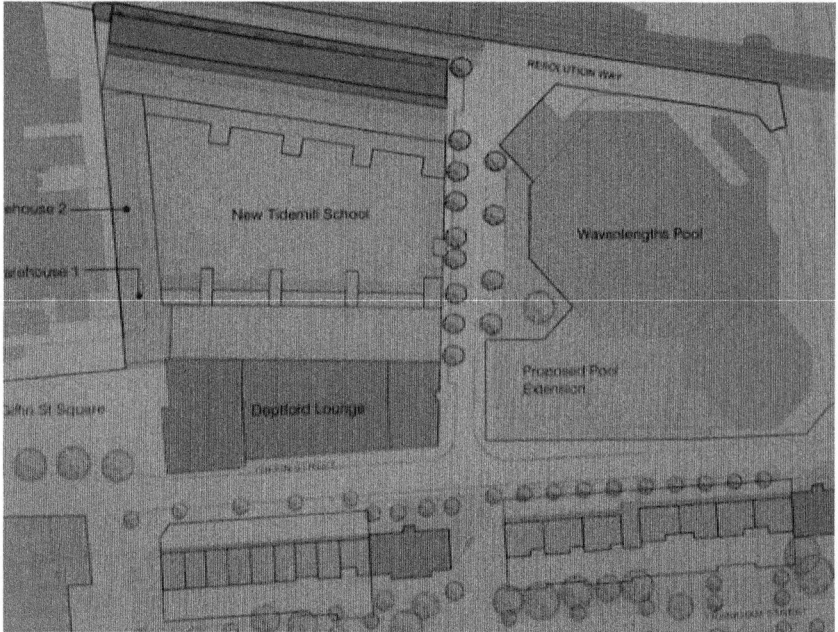

Site of community buildings on the former
Show Ground site and adjacent stone yard
© Pollard Thomas Edwards, photographer Robert Greshoff

By the time of the closure of the Show Ground in 1961 there was a much reduced programme. It was still enjoyed, however, by local children, teenagers and families whose pleasure in the rides, especially the Dodgems, the Bingo and the slot machines are recorded in *Chapter 4*.

Entrance to Tidemill Academy, incorporating the Show Ground house built by Charles Cain in 1913 behind the reception area, now used as offices. Courtesy of Tidemill Academy

The Deptford Lounge; *see entrance to Tidemill Academy on the left*
© Pollard, Thomas and Edwards Architects,
photographer Robert Greshoff

The story of Deptford Show Ground is the story of a lost world; as the last permanent fairground in London, it was one of many similar fairs throughout London and indeed the whole country. At a time before cinema, television and radio, it had an important function, providing nightly entertainment and a place to meet for the ordinary people of Deptford and beyond. *See Chapter 4 for memories of people in Deptford who enjoyed the Show Ground when they were children and Chapter 5 for the historical context.*

The lifestyle begun by Charles Cain towards the end of the nineteenth century has been continued by one branch of the Cain family still operating in the leisure industry on the South Coast. Run by the great grandchildren and great great grandsons of Charles Cain, 'Cain's Amusements' is now centred on Herne Bay and surrounding towns. *See Chapters 2, 3 and 5.*

Cain's Amusements, Herne Bay ©David Cain Senior

This history of the Deptford Show Ground has been put together from a number of sources, including Census and other official records, family photographs and documents and information from the National Fairground and Circus Archive at Sheffield University, including the Showmen's Guild archive, The Fairground Society, from press reports from contemporary newspapers and from the work of Fairground Historians Frances Brown, Kevin Scrivens and Stephen Smith.[4] First-hand accounts of travelling life by "Lord" George Sanger[5] and Frances Brown (a)[6] are drawn on for background information. First-hand memories of members of the Cain family are mainly in *Chapter 3*, and include photographs and anecdotes from an album compiled by Daisy Bell, *née* Cain, youngest daughter of Charles and Hannah for her grandsons and also from taped interviews from 1986.[7]

Notes and references

(1)   I have decided to use the term "showmen" to include all showmen instead of the politically correct terms "showwomen" and "show people" which are not in general usage. The usual spelling of "showground" is replaced by "Show Ground", or "Show Grounds", as it was written in Charles Cain's will and other documents.

(2)   *'Introduction'* by Kenneth Grahame to Seventy Years a Showman by "Lord" George Sanger, George Cruikshank, Mathew Crampton and Kenneth Grahame, Muddler Books, 2018.

(3)   As is usual in showmen's families there is a repetition of first names across the generations. To avoid confusion: "Charles Cain" bought the Show Ground; his son Charles is referred to as "Charlie". Charles' father is referred to as "Grandad David"; Charles' son is referred to as Dave; the remaining two David Cain's are then differentiated as David Cain Senior and David Cain Junior. Charles' son is referred to as Tom; Tom's great grandson is referred to as Tom Junior. Tom's son, Bill, is referred to as Stanley Bill and his grandson is simply "Bill". For the most part, the person referred to is clear from the context. Tracing the family back to 1715, there are two more Thomas Cain's recorded, one born in 1715 and one in 1735! Finally, both Hannah, wife of Charles Cain and their eldest daughter are called Hannah: I have chosen to refer to them both as "Hannah" as who is being referred to is clear from the context.

(4)   *'The Lost History of our Streets Deptford High Street'* by Stephen Smith in The Fairground Society magazine *'Platform'*, November, 2012.

(5)   Seventy Years a Showman, by "Lord" George Sanger, George Cruikshank, Mathew Crampton and Kenneth Grahame, Muddler Books. 2018.

(6)   Fairfield Folk, A history of the British Fairground and its People, Frances Brown, (a) 1986, Ronda Books.

(7)   Unpublished album by Daisy Bell and unpublished recordings of interviews by Harley Bell with his grandparents Daisy and Ernest Bell (1986).

Chapter Two

The Deptford Show Ground and the Cain family

Charles Cain and his father Grandad David came from a farming family in the Aylesbury, Buckinghamshire area; as a young man Charles and his father worked as agricultural labourers.[1] Like many before them, they were attracted to the bright lights and greater business opportunities within the travelling community of showmen; they became showmen selling fancy goods, progressing to many different fairground attractions, assisted by David's wife Ann, *née* Towersley, and Charles' wife Hannah, *née* Knighton, whose family had been showmen and travellers in London for several generations. By the time of the 1881 Census Charles was registered as a 'master carter', which meant that he now had his own horse and cart.

The photo on the next page is of the Cain family wagon, horse and tent, probably sold around the time Charles' mother Ann died in 1902, suggests the way the family would have travelled between fairgrounds in the early days.

The day of the sale of the old Cain family wagon and tent;
see the smoking chimney above the wagon ©Bell family archive

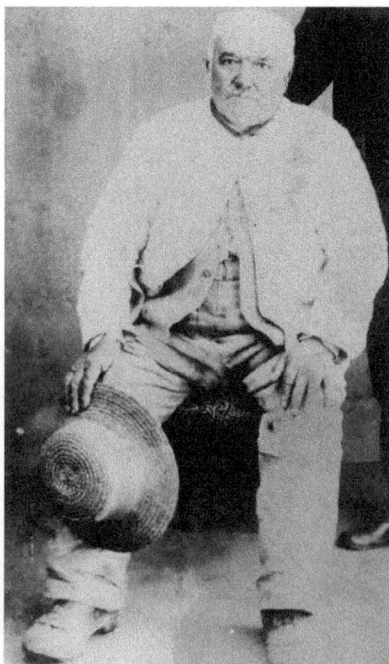

Grandad David and his wife Ann Cain, *née* Towersley
©Bell family archive

In 1884 Charles married Hannah Knighton, daughter of Elizabeth Irvin, *née* Young, and Thomas Knighton Senior, fellow showmen whose family is recorded as being on the Deptford Show Ground in 1891, as was Charles Cain and his family. Charles and Hannah went on to have eight children: Hannah (Dot), Charles (Charlie), David (Dave), Thomas (Tom), Frederick (Fred), Florence (Florrie), Carolyn (Carrie) and Daisy.

Hannah Knighton had one full brother, Thomas, and six half siblings, for her mother had married Thomas Knighton Senior after the death of her first husband, James Abraham Irvin, by whom she had six children – thereby creating a half-sibling link between the Cain's and the Irvin's – another well-known and prestigious family of showmen operating to this day throughout the U.K., trading under the name 'Irvin Leisure'.[2]

© Irvin Leisure

Charles was very ambitious and gradually became more prosperous, building up his 'cartering' business and also trying his hand at any fairground attractions that he thought would be successful and make money:

Dada [Charles] was quite a chap ... but generally speaking he was the ideas man. Poor old Muma [Hannah] was the one who had to do it all. In the rougher times he would concoct some kind of fairground act and hope for the best. Muma usually finished up as the act. He used her as the target in a knife-throwing act. Daisy Bell's unpublished album

By 1891 Charles was registered as a 'hawker and traveller' based on Census Day in a 'van' at the Railway Arches and Show Ground: 'part of a 'vibrant and fairly affluent travelling fairground community who had made Deptford a base for over 200 years'. *Stephen Smith.*[3] Indeed, Deptford High Street was thriving at this time. In 1898, William Booth, social reformer, described it as 'the Oxford Street of South East London' and noted that all the shopkeepers made enough money to be able to afford servants.[4]

Charles still retained his links with Aylesbury and by 1901 he was back there on Census Day, registered as a 'wholesale china dealer', probably supplying prizes to fellow showmen, as he was later to do on an ever bigger scale.

By 1911 Charles and Hannah were registered at 144 Deptford High Street on Census Day as a 'fancy goods dealer', supplying and distributing 'swag' (fairground prizes), while continuing to having a presence on the Show Ground with both 'joints' and rides (side shows and Gallopers).

Other showmen registered at the Show Ground in 1891, at the time of the Census, included Charles' brother-in-law, Dick Saunders, who in 1898 was advertising for freaks, novelties and curiosities 'for the best ground' in London. *Stephen Smith.*

Dick Saunders outside his wagon on the Show Ground in 1891
©Bell family archive

In 1899 Richard Pettigrove was advertising ground to let for 'respectable shows'. In 1900 a number of big attractions were recorded on the Show Ground:

- Swing Boats, owned by the Weatherhead family,
- Harris's Circus,
- Whiteley's Waxworks Exhibition,
- Henrietta Wilson's Gallopers,
- Gilbey's Rifle Saloon and Sheets,
- Harris' 'Emmas' and
- 'Emmas and Roll-downs' owned by Thomas Knighton Junior. *Stephen Smith.*

Two adverts placed in the *Era* newspaper illustrate how the well known showmen, the Biddall Brothers[5] were preparing for the 1901/2 winter season at the Show Ground:

Wanted, trapeze, Swinging Perch or Good Clairvoyant Show, open Monday, Show Ground, Deptford. Double turn preferred. No fancy prices. Amateurs save stamps.

Also they placed another advert for: 'musicians, a good E Flat Bass and a Cornet' (*Era*, 14th December 1901) *Frances Brown (b)*[(6)]

Biddall's American menagerie and a tightrope walker were the star attractions that winter at the Show Ground:

Amongst the acts were the North American Indian impalement act by the Brothers Biddall, followed by Captain Hunter who put the pack of Siberian wolves through their paces, concluding his act by placing his face in one of their mouths and feeding the pack from his hands. He then performed with two educated lions before presenting Brutus, the untameable lion. Only twelve months before Hunter had been mauled at Deptford when one of the lions knocked him down and tore away the flesh from his thigh. *Stephen Smith*

Biddall's were back at Deptford in March 1902 after moving from the Showground first to Peckham and then Battersea. From Battersea they advertised for a new lion tamer for their Cinematograph show at the Show Ground:

Wanted, Lion Tamer, Black or White, also Good Doorsman that understands working Living Pictures and Two Knockabouts. Must be strictly sober and attentive to business. Young men only of good appearance. Biddall's Animated Pictures, Deptford. *Era,* 15th March, 1902.

By February 1903 they were more specific about wanting a lion tamer of colour:

'Wanted, Lion Tamer, Coloured Man preferred'. *Era*, 28th February 1903. *See Chapter 5.*

By early 1903 they had engaged extra talent in the person of 'Great Blondon' who nightly walked from one end of the Show Ground to the other on a rope forty foot high and 'Crypto', a strong boy who performed 'remarkable feats of lifting and pulling'.

But by 1904–05. Biddall's were disposing of their menagerie as travelling animal acts were going out of fashion and also criticised in the press for cruelty to animals:

Wanted to sell, 5 waggons of Wild Beasts...including Two Lionesses (Performing), One Full grown Lion... Four Male Performing Wolves, One Striped Hyena, One Bear, and One Female Wolf, Ten Monkeys, and a variety of other Animals and Birds. The whole of the above are in the pink of condition. For price and particulars, address...High Street, Deptford. *The Era*, 2nd January 1904, *Frances Brown (b).*

Biddall's used their extended stay at the Show Ground to construct a new Bioscope show, with moving pictures, for the new season, along with 'Roberts' Mysteries', 'Hastings' midgets' and 'Miss Lambert, the Leicester giantess':

[The new Bioscope] was fronted by a magnificent gilt, wood and plaster facade with brightly painted panels, the broad wooden steps leading up to its pay box being flanked by two ornate pillars. Inside it was equipped with a screen and projector capable of providing the public with the very latest 'entertainment'. *Frances Brown (b)*

Biddall's new Bioscope; John Biddall is "dooring"
Courtesy of Frances Brown

Biddall's continued to innovate and develop more and more exciting shows, but by 1912 they were selling their Cinematograph equipment and films – they could no longer compete with competition from permanent cinema halls that were proving very popular by this time.

Biddall's also had competition from Alf Ball, another celebrated and innovative showman, who was based at the Show Ground from 1905 and used it as his permanent address. Here is a picture of his Cinematograph that he adapted from his earlier Bioscope. While at the Show Ground in 1906 he took delivery of his new Burrell steam engine 'Alfred the Great'. The same year, when 'Alfred the Great' broke down, Ball decided to transport his Cinematograph between distant fairgrounds on the London and North Western Railway: a spark from the engine unfortunately set fire to the show front, causing £75 worth of damage to the carved work and paintings.[7]

Alf Ball's Cinematograph on the Exhibition Ground
©The Fairground Society

In March 1902, Charles Gilbey, Charles Cain and Frank Knighton Junior were on the Show Ground alongside Biddall's with their 'games'. These included: 'Jack Hastings' Fat Lady Show' featuring 'Beautiful Violet – a living, walking, talking mountain of fat' and 'Storey's Fine Art Gallery'. 'Harry Hughes Assault at Arms Boxing Show' was also a major attraction.[8] *Stephen Smith.* There were also local Deptford people who boxed at the Showground. *See Chapter 4.*

Joe Bowker, bantam weight champion of the world in 1904 and 1905, fought with Harry Hughes Boxing

Show at the Show Ground. Joe is said to have defeated over sixty opponents in four years from the age of 16. British Boxing Historian Maurice Golesworthy had this to say about Bowker's skills:

> Indeed, there are many authorities who rate Joe Bowker as the most skilful boxer ever produced in this country. That may be an exaggeration but it is safe to say that there have been few better. *Wikipedia*[9]

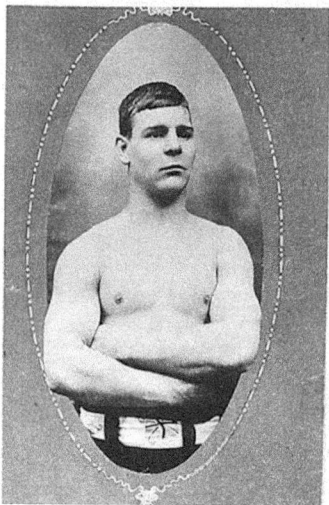

Jo Bowker, champion boxer
© Wikipedia

Charles Cain is recorded as having side shows on the Show Ground at this time in successive years, but no big rides: 'Games were provided by Messrs. Gilbey, Cain and Knighton Junior'. Side shows included:

- 'The Petrified Woman',
- 'Midget Kangaroos',
- 'A Giant Rat' and a
- 'Temple of Parisian Pleasures'.

In 1908 patents for C. Beech's 'Aeroplanes', that could be viewed at the Deptford Exhibition Ground or at Scotland Rd Liverpool, were advertised in the *World's Fair*:

The New Money Takers

Beech's Patent Aeroplanes.

This Machine is a great success...They can take money twice as fast as ordinary Machines...They are a sweet ride, do not make people sick, and the more people ride the more they want to...the roughest of the rough can do them no harm. *World's Fair* newspaper, 1st February, 1908.

By 1912 Charles' 'swag' business, supplying china and glass, sweets, chocolates and confetti to fairs across southern England, was so successful that he had enough money to buy the freehold of the Show Ground from Mrs. Weatherhead[10]. He went on to build a large warehouse on the site from which to sell and distribute the swag, as well as a detached house built in 1913–14 by Charles Moore, Florence Cain's father-in-law.

Ten years later Charles bought extra land – a stone yard on Giffin Street – which he later let to the Council on a 99-year lease and left to his sons in his will:

The Stone Yard was even bigger than the Show Ground. He [Charles] let that on a 99-year lease to the local Council and they had all different kinds and all different colours [of stones] in piles. They [my brothers] sold it for £20,000. Daisy Bell's *unpublished recordings.*

In 1991 Wavelengths Leisure Centre built by Lewisham Council opened on the site of the old stone yard:[11]

Wavelengths Leisure pool ©Greenwich Leisure Ltd.

It seems likely that Charles Cain made the majority of his money from selling swag while acting as 'riding master', having his own rides and stalls and sub-letting part of the Show Ground to other showmen, particularly to family and friends. Charles' swag business would probably have taken a downturn during the First World War, however, as many travelling fairs were stopped from operating by the Government of the day, so there would have been less need for prizes. *Frances Brown (a).*[12]

Charles and Hannah Cain in 1909 with their sons Fred, Tom, Dave and Charlie (back row) and daughters Hannah, Daisy, Florence and Carolyn (l to r) ©Bell family archive

Born in 1905, Daisy would have been 6 or 7 when her father bought the Show Ground. Here are her memories of the house and warehouse being built.

There was always a buzz of talk in the kitchen because I had four brothers. They were all at home in this High Street shop [144 High Street], they were men: Charlie was 19 years older than me. After it had been bought then came the excitement of building the warehouse [in 1912]...Then I can remember the house being started [in 1913]. There were great discussions about how the stairs were going to be put up. The great thing was that it had to be built tall to save 'tober' [space on the fairground]...because of all the roundabouts and stalls built up on the Grounds. Between the house and the warehouse there was a scullery, a wash house and a toilet. Daisy Bell, unpublished recordings.

Charles still retained his love of travelling and even after he had built his house on the Show Ground, he liked to sleep in his fairground 'wagon' in the summer months. *Daisy Bell's unpublished album.*

Amazingly, the exterior walls of both the Show Ground house and the warehouse still exist today and have been thoughtfully incorporated into the state-of-art school building of Tidemill Academy, designed by Pollard, Thomas and Edwards Architects. The house has been turned into offices with a modern lift up the centre of the building. The ground floor of the warehouse has been turned into classrooms with a staff room upstairs; *see the original beams in the photograph of the staff room.*

Close up of exterior of classrooms and staffroom at Tidemill
Academy built on the shell of the Show Ground warehouse
©Pollard, Thomas and Edwards Architects

View of the classrooms and staffroom at Tidemill Academy built
from the Show Ground warehouse; see *the edge of the Show Ground
house on the left.* Courtesy of Tidemill Academy.

Tidemill Academy staff room showing the original beams of
the Show Ground warehouse.
Courtesy of Tidemill Academy

Charles' four sons and extended family all helped to run the family business, especially his sons Charlie (1887–1968), Dave (1888–1940) Tom (1890–1966) and Fred (1892–1928).

The four Cain boys in 1909: Charlie, Dave, Tom and Fred (l to r)
©Bell family archive

Sadly, Fred died in 1928, following 'a long "and troublesome" illness', believed to be tuberculosis, prevalent at that time in London. *See pp. 32–33 and Daisy's memories in Chapter 3.* The business passed to Charles' sons Dave, Tom and Charlie on the death of their father in 1935. Dave, died in 1940 from 'catching a blighty' – gassed in the trenches during the First World War. *See Daisy's memories in Chapter 3.* Dave's untimely death left Tom and Charlie in charge of the Show Ground through to its closure in 1961.

Charles and Hannah's daughters were also expected to help out while they lived at home, particularly during the First World War, when there was a shortage of labour. They mostly went on to marry out of the showmen's world: the eldest daughter, Hannah (1886–1952) married Alfred Parrish, publican of the Green Man pub in Catford; Florence (1894–1989) married Charles Moore, a builder; Carolyn (1900–1979) married George Corey, a painter and decorator, who worked on the Show Ground for 40 years as a driver; and the youngest daughter, Daisy, (1905–1996) who married Ernest Bell, a butcher. *See Chapter 3 for Daisy's memories, those of Florence's daughter, Dorothy, and Hannah's great grandson, Ian Wake.*

There are family anecdotes of both Daisy and Carolyn working on rides as young women, especially on the new Gallopers, which were a major attraction at the time. Daisy told her grandson, Harley, that she had worked collecting fares from the paying public and that the shifts were long and tiring because of all the "jumping on and off". Michael Flatt remembers visiting the Show Ground at the age of 5 or 6 and being shown around by his Grandad George (Corey) and his Grandma Carolyn proudly sharing with him how she had worked on the Gallopers as a teenager. Here is a picture of Carolyn on the Gallopers in 1916 or thereabouts when she would have been 16. *See Daisy's evocative memories of working on the Gallopers in Chapter 3.*

Carolyn Cain 'minding' the Gallopers – giving a ride to Alfie Parrish (son of Hannah Parrish, *née* Cain) c. 1916 ©Bell family archive

As well as fare collectors and a driver on the Gallopers, the family also employed Wally, an 'organ boy':

Wally ©Bell family archive

In the good old days, when staff were relatively easy to come by, most rides with organs on them had someone who was working on the organ full time to put the folded cardboard music books through the key frame of the organ. Each tune was on a separate book, so when a tune finished, a new book had to be fed into the key frame, and the old book put back into the wooden boxes that the book music was stored in. Most tunes were less than 5 minutes, so it was quite time consuming, and at busy times the fare collectors and the driver wouldn't have time to change the books on the organ,

Key frame from
a Gavioli organ
©The Fairground Society

and a ride is nothing without the organ playing. It would usually be an older member of staff, or as in Cain's case, a young boy. Kevin Scrivens, unpublished information.

George Corey, husband of Carolyn, née Cain,
standing by Cain's 87-key Gavioli organ
©The Fairground Society

The Gallopers would have been a major investment for the family in 1915. They were regarded as state-of-the-art and iconic; they replaced an earlier set of Gallopers the family sold in 1916[13]. Built by Savages of Kings Lynn, they were named 'Colonial Gallopers': they were delivered to the Show Ground decorated in the flags of Great Britain and her World War I allies. Charles' cousin, Joe Saunders (son of Dick Saunders), drove it for many years, naming its steam engine 'Britains Pride'. The new Gallopers were sold in 1954 to Botton Brothers in Great Yarmouth, where they are still in use at the Great Yarmouth Pleasure Beach.[14] *Daisy Bell, unpublished album.*

The first photo on the next page shows the original order for the Gallopers. Bought for £1587, this approximates to £145,000 in 2022.

© Cain family archive

Peggy Corey, daughter of Carolyn Corey, *née* Cain,
visiting the Gallopers at Great Yarmouth in the 1970s
www.pleasure-beach.co.uk/history.html ©Corey family archive

Charles' swag business continued to expand. 'Cain's Amusements' vans bearing a transfer of galloping horses on red doors became a familiar sight throughout Southern England after the First World War, replacing the horse and cart of earlier days:

Some [swag] was distributed by train and some by road in the family's first Ford XA 3434 driven by Dave Cain, George Corey and Harry Irvin.[15] Daisy Bell's unpublished album.

Cain drivers posing by Charles Cain's lorry in about 1921
©Bell family archive

George [Corey] was in charge of one of these vans and, for example, he would be at Oxford late at night after the fair had closed and taking orders and return with them to Deptford. The night staff in the large warehouse would make the orders up and have three lorry loads ready to go to Oxford at 6 a.m. the next morning. Undated news item from the World's Fair newspaper, cited by Daisy Bell.

Up until the First World War, the Cain family reportedly bought much of their swag from Germany, subsequently buying it from the Potteries in Stoke and elsewhere:

Before the First World War everything came from Germany or Austria. Everything I remember in Dada's warehouse said 'Made in Bavaria'. One of the things that he used to stock was silver and glass vases. At one time I don't think there was a house in Deptford that didn't have one of these or a pair. I think they cost 4½d [four-and-a-half old pence, 2p in today's money]. *Later on he had 'Staffordshire's' that they used to send out as swag. "They [cost] nothing ..."* Daisy Bell's unpublished recordings. See Chapter 3.

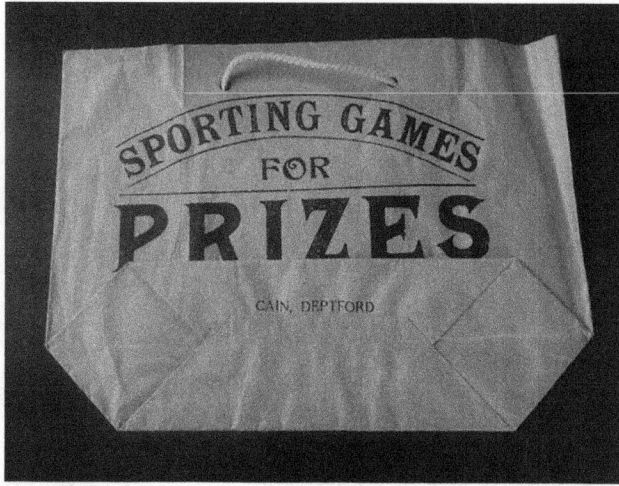

Cain, Deptford paper carrier bag ©Bell family archive

The Show Ground had strong links with the Showmen's Guild of Great Britain, an organisation set up in 1890 to protect the rights and further the interests of showmen.[16] C. Whitehead was a member from 1900 and also other showmen associated with the Show Ground: H and C. Irvin, Forrest Brothers, Frank Bailey, Alf Ball and Thomas Knighton Senior; "Lord" George Sanger was the President and a founder member. The Cain's waited until 1908 to sign up – Charles Cain paying 5 shillings for the privilege. By this time the Guild had split into regional organisations and they were able to join the London Section (1907). The family threw themselves into the work of the Guild: Charlie was Secretary of the London Section from 1920, Dave became Treasurer from 1933 to his death in 1940. Fred was Assistant Secretary and Charlie and Fred were auditors (from 1927). Fred's obituary in the *World's Fair* in October 1928 was fulsome in its praise of him and his role within the Showmen's Guild:

Fred Cain was a member of the London Section of the Showmen's Guild...for a number of years. A most conscientious worker and at unravelling facts that had not been properly put before conferences or meetings he certainly did excel...he would stand and ask for some little point to be put clearly before the members assembled together. He read the rule books so often and consistently that he could quote from memory the passage that had any bearing on the point in dispute.

Fred Cain ©Bell family archive

The family all enjoyed the social aspect of the Guild as well as the business side: Dave was Chairman of the Guild's Amateur Football Club; annual Showmen's Guild dinner dances were an opportunity to dress up and party and meet with wider family and friends.

In common with other prominent showmen of the day, Charles Cain and his sons were also all active Masons and indeed Charlie, Tom, Dave and brother-in-law George Corey set up the Deptford Lodge of Instruction.[17]

Freemasonry would have given them both a moral/spiritual compass and a means of connecting with other local business people. They were proud of their roles within the Masonic structure and the whole family looked forward to annual Masonic 'ladies nights' (dinner/dances) that they took turns to organise when they took on the role of 'Grand Master'.

Freemasonry is an ancient system designed to impart morality and ethics and teach mutual service to its members. Masonry seeks to make good individuals better through education, improvement, and service. While containing religious elements, Masonry is also a fraternal organization that encourages morality, charity, and philosophical studies. It has no clergy, no sacraments, nor a prescribed path of salvation. Moreover, Masonry rejects dogma and inspires individuals to utilize reason to search for Truth. *The Masonic Philosophical Society.*

Family members at the inauguration of the Deptford School of Instruction: George Corey (centre back row) Charlie, Tom and Dave Cain (front row) ©Bell family archive

There were strong links between other fairs and the Deptford Show Ground, as showmen regularly travelled between different fairs, especially in the summer; in particular, the prestigious 3-day Mitcham Fair where over 600 showmen gathered with their rides and stalls from all parts of the country from 12th to 14th August each year. Charlie Cain was recorded as being the auditor of Mitcham Fair from 1920.[16] The Cain family was especially proud to hold the ceremonial key at the Deptford Show Ground that each year was fetched by a new Mayor of Mitcham at the start of the fair in August. *Daisy Bell's album.* The Showmen's Guild became involved as mediators in the early 1920s when the showmen of Mitcham fell out with the local community 'Conservators', who deemed it noisy and a nuisance and wanted to ban it. The showmen ended up being forced to change the site of the fair. *Frances Brown (a)* The Cain's would have been involved in this dispute due to their roles as Guild officers.[18]

Dave Cain with the new mayor of Mitcham on Cain's Gallopers proudly holding his golden key to open the Mitcham Fair; *undated and unattributed newspaper cutting from Daisy Bell's album* ©Bell family archive

Mitcham Fair 1924; meeting from Alf Ball's Bioscope Show,
addressed by Rev Thomas Horne, (centre with white beard)
Chaplain and Organiser of the Showmen's Guild, with members of
Mitcham Council, discussing the potential abolition of the fair
©Merton Libraries

By the 1930s, the side shows at the Ground would have included Bingo, juke boxes, a shooting gallery, a boxing booth, slot machines and anything deemed likely to make money, rather than the freak shows, menageries and moving picture shows of earlier times. With the exception of the boxing booths[19], most of these side shows remained popular and would have remained on the Ground until the end of the 1950s. *See Daisy Bell's and my memories in Chapter 3 and also Chapter 4.*

In 1933, the family had packed up its iconic Gallopers, probably because they took up a lot of room and were by now out of fashion: people were drawn to faster, more thrilling rides such as Arks and Skids (see photos in Chapter 3) and Dodgems (see photo in Chapter 4). *Frances Brown (a).* Indeed, in 1939 the family bought a set of Dodgems supplied by Lakins, that remained on the Show Ground up until just before its closure in 1961.

Charles became so successful that by the time he died in 1935 at the age of 74, his estate and legacies were worth the equivalent of several millions of pounds in today's money. He was well regarded in Deptford:

The deceased was very popular in the district and had won a reputation for honesty in business and fair-dealing and for being charitable towards all worthy causes. *Charles' obituary in the World's Fair, 1935.*

Much of Charles' wealth must have been derived from his wholesale business and he often chose to refer to himself as a 'china and glass' or 'earthenware' merchant, rather than a showman. His wealth enabled him to buy a number of newly-built terraced houses for his children throughout Deptford, some of which were demolished during the so-called 'slum clearance' in the 1960s. *See Ian Wake's memories in Chapter 3.*

TIDEWAY 1649.

Bought of

CHARLES CAIN BROS.
(PARTNERS: C. CAIN, D. CAIN, T. CAIN)

CHINA, GLASS AND FANCY GOODS,
102a. DEPTFORD HIGH STREET, LONDON. S.E.8

TERMS CASH.   Place Orders Early for Bank Holidays.

Headed invoice paper probably in use from 1935 to 1940
©Cain family archive

The Second World War must have been a challenging time for the family: not only would they have had the stress of constant bombardments affecting Deptford, they would have found it hard to find staff. It was also a time of personal tragedy for the family. Dave Cain died in 1940, leaving a widow, Ada Gertrude, *née* Richards, and a 16-year-old daughter, Vera. Then, in May 1942, Charlie's son Barry, a Sergeant Navigator in the R.A.F., was killed in an air sortie over Norway. *See Chapter 5.*

Charlie's first wife Edith Lucy Cain, *née* Faulkner, sadly died the following year in April 1943. Charles' wife Hannah died at the age of 79 in 1946. She was well known and popular throughout Deptford. Here is an extract from her obituary published in the *World's Fair*.

Hundreds of people from all over Deptford and far beyond knew Mrs. Hannah Cain, the cheery, good-hearted proprietress of the fairground at 102a Deptford High Street...All the morning family and friends were bringing floral tributes to the silent fair ground and scores of wreaths transformed the area normally merry with bumper-cars into a colourful garden sacred to her memory. *World's Fair, March, 1946*

Other fairground families continued until the late 1950s to rent space on the Show Ground when their travelling fairs closed down in the winter. A number of well known show families stayed on the Grounds or had their rides there at different times: Bailey's, Knighton's, Wilson's, Forrest's, Thurston's – many of whose descendents are still working as showmen.

Daisy Cain, aged 15, on Wilson's Switchback at the Show Ground in 1920
that is now part of the Fairground Heritage Trust collection in
Devon ©Bell family archive

Hannah Cain hanging out her washing on a set of Gondolas owned
by the Thurston family, circa 1925 ©Bell family archive

When Charles died in 1935, Tom, Charlie and Dave
inherited the Show Ground, although they had been
effectively running it between them for some years, under
the sometimes iron hand of their father. By the time of its
closure on 25 March 1961, the Show Ground had lost

momentum – although it was still appreciated by local people right up to its closure. *See Chapter 4.*

Tom and Charlie were by now elderly (aged 71 and 74, respectively) and lacked the energy to innovate; there were no family members able to take the Show Ground forward. Neither did it fit with the vision of a new post-war Deptford envisioned by the planners. It was compulsorily purchased by Lewisham Council for what was regarded by the family as a very meagre sum, believed to be £3000 - £64,400 at today's prices (in 2022).

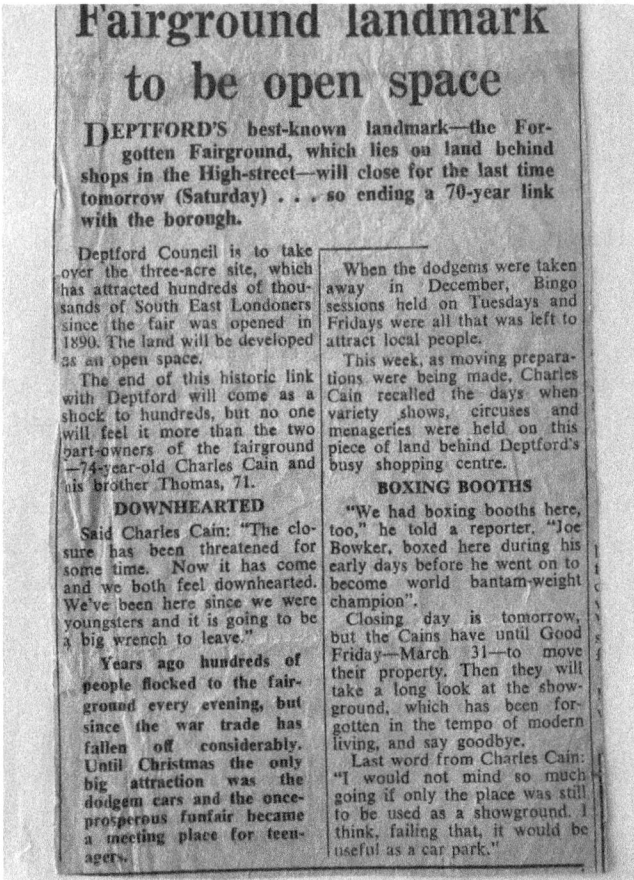

Fairground landmark to be open space

DEPTFORD'S best-known landmark—the Forgotten Fairground, which lies on land behind shops in the High-street—will close for the last time tomorrow (Saturday) . . . so ending a 70-year link with the borough.

Deptford Council is to take over the three-acre site, which has attracted hundreds of thousands of South East Londoners since the fair was opened in 1890. The land will be developed as an open space.

The end of this historic link with Deptford will come as a shock to hundreds, but no one will feel it more than the two part-owners of the fairground —74-year-old Charles Cain and his brother Thomas, 71.

DOWNHEARTED

Said Charles Cain: "The closure has been threatened for some time. Now it has come and we both feel downhearted. We've been here since we were youngsters and it is going to be a big wrench to leave."

Years ago hundreds of people flocked to the fairground every evening, but since the war trade has fallen off considerably. Until Christmas the only big attraction was the dodgem cars and the once-prosperous funfair became a meeting place for teenagers.

When the dodgems were taken away in December, Bingo sessions held on Tuesdays and Fridays were all that was left to attract local people.

This week, as moving preparations were being made, Charles Cain recalled the days when variety shows, circuses and menageries were held on this piece of land behind Deptford's busy shopping centre.

BOXING BOOTHS

"We had boxing booths here, too," he told a reporter. "Joe Bowker, boxed here during his early days before he went on to become world bantam-weight champion".

Closing day is tomorrow, but the Cains have until Good Friday—March 31—to move their property. Then they will take a long look at the showground, which has been forgotten in the tempo of modern living, and say goodbye.

Last word from Charles Cain: "I would not mind so much going if only the place was still to be used as a showground. I think, failing that, it would be useful as a car park."

Cutting from the *Kentish Mercury* newspaper, 24th March 1961

A sad end to the Show Ground: the double gates were no more,
'their lights twinkling, signalling the opening of the Show Ground'
since the 1930s

Following the closure of the Show Ground, it was used as a car park for a number of years. Tom and Charlie were upset by the sale of the Show Ground, their entire focus for their adult lives, although they no longer lived in Deptford, travelling daily from their homes in Beckenham and Forest Hill respectively.

Tom with his wife Rose in November 1959 at a Masonic dinner dance
©Cain family archive

Charlie Cain with his fiancée Jean Devitt in 1961 ©Bell family archive

Despite the closure of the Show Ground, both its name and traditions have been proudly continued by one branch of the Cain family, operating on the South Coast. Yes, 'Cain's Amusements', set up by the late Stanley Bill Cain and his wife Frances, *née* Bailey, is still a thriving leisure business in the seaside resorts of Cliftonville, Herne Bay, Sheerness and Leysdown. Stanley Bill, younger son of Tom Cain, and grandson of Charles and Hannah

Cain, married Frances Bailey in 1953; Stanley Bill joined Frances' family who were following a traditional showman lifestyle travelling between fairs throughout Kent and South London (Forrest and Bailey), where they were according to Stephen Smith *"significant players"*.[20] The family stopped travelling in the late 1960s and put down roots in Dover and later in Herne Bay, where they bought the Pier Arcade. Frances and Bill had met at the Show Ground where Frances' family opened two of their rides there during the winter – an Ark and a Skid.

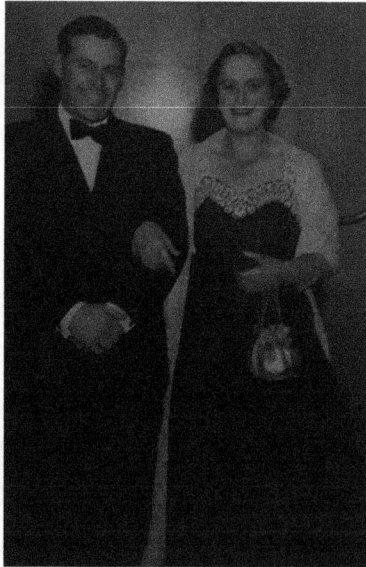

Stanley Bill and Frances Cain at a Showmen's
Guild dinner dance in the 1950s.
©Bell family archive

When Frances sadly died in 1987 and Stanley Bill in 2016, it was a huge blow to the family. Their expanding and thriving business is now run by fourth and fifth generation of Cain showmen: David Senior, his wife Tracy, sons David Junior, Bill and Tom Junior and sisters Francesca and Rosanne. *See Chapter 3 for David and Rosanne's memories and Chapter 5 for discussion of Francesca, Rosanne and Tracy's role in the business.*

The latest generation of Cain showmen: Tom Junior,
Bill and David Junior (l to r)
©David Cain Senior

CELEBRATING 40 YEARS IN HERNE BAY 1977 - 2017
CAIN'S AMUSEMENTS
SAVE THE DATE 7/10/17

©David Cain Senior

Notes and references

(1)   Census Information – Charles Cain

    1871 Scholar – Aylesbury
    1881 Master carter – Aylesbury (carter=conveyor of goods in a cart; 'master' denotes ownership of a cart)
    1891 Railway arches Show Ground Deptford – Hawker and traveller
    1901 Wholesale china dealer, Aylesbury
    1911 Fancy goods dealer, Deptford

(2)   www.irvinleisure.co.uk.

(3)   'The Lost History of our Streets Deptford High Street' by Stephen Smith in The Fairground Society magazine *'Platform'*, November, 2012.

(4)   William Booth, social reformer, cited by Wikipedia.

(5)   Biddolph's Show was managed by Bert Jervis who operated the Cinematograph machine imported from America. Among the films shown were "The Road to Ruin", "The Prodigal Son'" and "Scrooge". *Stephen Smith*

(6)   Brown, Frances (b), Fairground Strollers and Showfolk, Ronda Books, 2001.

(7)   National Fairground Archive Fact Sheet *'Bioscope Presenters Alf Ball'*.

(8)   Part of a long tradition of boxing events in travelling fairs going back to bare knuckle boxing before 1867 when new 'Queensbury rules' enabled greater protection for participants. Denis Fleming, The Manchester Fighters, Neil Richardson, Manchester, 1986.

(9)   Maurice Golesworthy, The Encyclopaedia of Boxing, Robert Hale, London, 1960, pp 35–36 cited by Wikipedia.

(10)   The Weatherhead family came from Lewisham; in the 1851 Census James Weatherhead was recorded as being a dustman; by 1861 he and his wife Harriet were recorded as 'toy dealers'. *Stephen Smith*

(11)   Wavelengths Leisure Centre was opened by Lewisham Council in 1991 and in 2020 it was taken over by Greenwich Leisure Ltd, a

non-profit charitable Social Enterprise organisation. It underwent an £800,000 refurbishment in 2021 following a campaign to save it from closure.

(12) Frances Brown (a) Fairfield Folk, A history of the British Fairground and its People, 1986, Ronda Books.

(13) The first set of Gallopers, known as 'Old Sookie', was acquired from George Baker of Southampton and was driven by a Burrell traction centre engine. In March 1915 Charles Cain advertised it for sale in the *World's Fair*:

Three abreast Gallopers, with 18 horses, 12 cockerels and two carriages, traction centre by Burrells, mounted on springs, double step platform, twisted brass, top and bottom centre droppers all complete. Reason for selling, going in for a different machine. *Stephen Smith, unpublished information.*

'Gallopers' are also known as 'Carousels'.

(14) Bottons Pride Gallopers http://www.pleasure-beach.co.uk/history. html:

This Savages 47-foot diameter, 3-abreast Gallopers set arrived on the park with Botton Bros in 1954. Built in 1914/15 for Charles Cain of Deptford, it was called the 'Colonial Galloping Horses'. Many of the horses are reputedly the carved originals and the centre engine is still in place although not used to power the ride. This 36 horse set holds pride of place by the entrance to the park. *www.gallopers at the Amusement Park. page 3.*

(15) Harry Irvin was born William Henry Withers in 1879; his father Henry Withers died a month before he was born. His mother Ada married John Irvin over a year later and he was then adopted by John; he retained his birth name on legal documents. *Kevin Scrivens unpublished information.* Harry Irvin was the father of Ada Irvin Junior a distant cousin and great friend of Daisy Bell. *See Daisy's memories* in *Chapter 3.*

(16) The Showmen's Guild of Great Britain, NFCA Archive; Showmen's Guild Year Books.

(17) Masonic schools of instruction "help Master Masons make the invisible visible, the hidden in plain view, and the art of our ritual

apparent to those who seek it. In order to attend any Masonic School of Instruction, you must be a Master Mason in good standing within your Lodge and present a current dues card upon registration." Masonic Philosophical Society.

(18) Showmen's Guild Year Book.

(19) In 1947 the Boxing Board of Control banned its licensed members from competing in fairground boxing booths. NFCA research article: *'Fairground shows – a history of the nineteenth century.'*

(20) Francis Bailey (1837–1902) great grandfather of Frances Cain, *née* Bailey, co-ran the prestigious annual World's Fair at the Agricultural Hall, Islington each winter, as well as having his own travelling fair. *Stephen Smith, unpublished information.*

Chapter Three

The Cain family remembers

Memories of
the late Daisy Bell, *née* Cain (1905–1996)
youngest daughter of Charles and Hannah Cain

Daisy Bell's memories are drawn from an album of anecdotes, newspaper cuttings and photographs she made for her two grandsons Bruce and Harley in 1979 and also from tape recordings she made with her husband Ernest and Harley in 1986 talking about her memories of the Show Ground and living on Deptford High Street. A number of Daisy's memories are also contained in Chapter 2, and include obituaries from the 'World's Fair' newspaper.

Daisy Bell with her two grandsons
Bruce and Harley Bell (l to r) in the 1980s.
©Bell family archive

Born in 1905, Daisy had vivid memories both of growing up on the Show Ground and also of the shop that the family had on Deptford High Street, where they sold swag, before they bought the Show Ground in 1912. As the youngest daughter of Hannah and Charles, Daisy was proud to be their only child to have been born at the High Street shop.

We were at 144 [Deptford High Street] in this shop. I was born there. It went right through from the High Street. It had a big shop where Dada had his office and then it went through to the packing department at the back right through to an opening, a long passage, in Crossfield Lane where there were two doors where he could get packing cases delivered.

144 Deptford High Street as it looks today. Courtesy of Tony's Daily

According to Daisy, her brothers Tom and Dave were "the best packers". She described how the big packing cases would be taken to the station in the family's horse and cart in the early days and how her mother was responsible for the planning and organising:

Harry Irvin took the big packing cases up to the station on a trolley [pulled by] a horse named Peggy. This mare was the pride of my Dada's life. My mother always knew which station they had to go to. She did the bills, she knew all the stations and where the trains ran.

Daisy remembered the very first night when the family moved onto the Show Ground in the Spring of 1914:

The first night on the Show Ground Dada sat with me by my bedside, because I'd got to get used to the organ playing on the roundabout. I was eight. The first roundabout he bought was 'Old Sookie' that he bought from Mr. Baker and that would be playing...Eventually I couldn't get to sleep unless it was playing...It was made by Gavioli, the Italian organ maker.

Just three years later Daisy was herself working on the big new Gallopers, delivered to the Show Ground in 1916 when she was just eleven years old. *See also Chapter 2.*

The War had started, you couldn't get money collectors. I started by minding one of the joints [stalls]. From there, we got so short of money takers I was easily collecting fares when I was 11 with Ada Irvin, my best friend.[1] *My sister Carolyn took the money on weekdays and Mama was taking the money on busy nights, Saturdays. In the busy time on Saturday... they did what they called 'cutting it up'. The engine driver was given the wheeze and you didn't go round many times. So you didn't have a lot of time to collect your fares. So Ada Irvin and I were allotted 6 horses each, it was a three abreast roundabout, and we used to follow one another. In order to know where your horses started, because you had to jump off, we used to have red, white and blue and on Saturdays, yellow. My 6 horses started it with red. It was just a piece of art muslin tied round the brass rail that you held to jump on. After my six horses it would be white and after that the men would have three or four lots: one would have blue and the next one yellow.*

The First World War was a powerful memory for Daisy: especially the zeppelin raids[2] and also a huge and terrifying explosion at Silvertown[3] in 1917, which resulted in all the windows being blown out of the Show Ground house and all along the High Street. Daisy's father, 'a country man', had been very frightened of the zeppelin raids and the explosion at Silvertown that could clearly be seen over the Show Ground. He decided to protect the house by stuffing the loft full of confetti to try and save it from a possible fire:

Dada had such a fear of fire, he used to sell sacks of confetti to the showmen. He said 'I'm selling no more confetti, we'll have it all in the loft'. So it was all stacked up, tons and tons of confetti. If the bombs fell direct he thought it would soften the blow and take time to get through all this confetti. Things were so short during and after the War, there was no paper, they couldn't make confetti so after the War he'd got bags and bags of confetti that nobody else had got. You can imagine the value of them after they were stacked. If you went to a fair when they were celebrating when the war was all over, the showmen could get any price you liked for a small bag of confetti that the boys and girls used to throw at each other and Dada had the stock of them.

Armistice Day, in 1918, signalling the end of World War I, was an important memory:

We shut up the roundabout quickly so that there wouldn't be any fireworks come down on the tilt, on the red, white and blue tilt [canvas roof] ...it cost £500, a fortune in those days. I was collecting money on the roundabout with my best friend and cousin Ada Irvin...My favourite brother Fred collected us up and off we went to Hilly Fields where all day they had been building this huge bonfire where there were fireworks.

Daisy believed the War was the start of her Dada's poor health, seeing him as of a nervous disposition. The next photograph shows him in front of the warehouse in a wheelchair in later life due to heart problems.

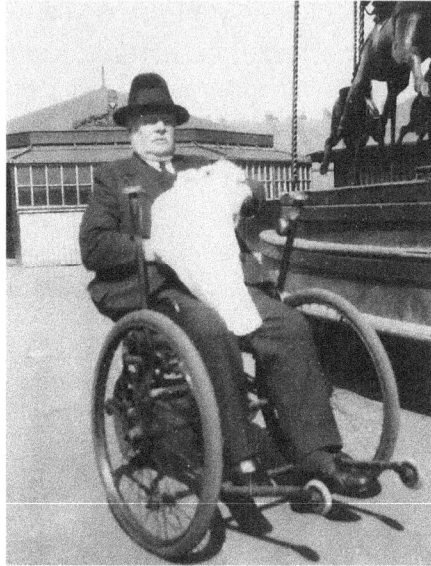

Charles Cain holding his youngest grandson Peter Bell in 1931,
four years before his death. *See the Bingo Hall in the background and
Gallopers to the right.* ©Bell family archive

A pullin' ball table
Courtesy of Kevin Scrivens

Daisy had a clear memory of the stalls and rides on the
Show Ground, especially those run by family members:

The first thing in the Grounds as you went down this long alleyway, (we called it "the Avenue") on the right was Ada Irvin's stall.[(4)] It was a "pullin ball" stall. "A penny a go". Everyone used to pull it hard and the ball used to fly around and go in one of the bottom compartments – they were known as "Shysters". The prize was a pair of boot laces or something like that. You got a prize every time. You got better prizes in the middle where it was very difficult – what they called the "top 'ole" prizes. These are three of the original "top 'ole" [prizes] from the stall: Ramsbotham, Enoch and Mr. Lovejoy.

Courtesy of Peter Bell ©Bell family archive

Daisy spoke about her brother Fred having a circular bicycle ride and also a football joint:

Fred had a football joint [stall] with skittles on that used to stand on 10 posts. You had to kick the football and knock one of these skittles off straight. You couldn't hit the back, it couldn't rebound. The profit wasn't too bad, though it wasn't good, because people got the hang of it. But blow me, there came somebody who was a trainer down at Millwall [Football Club] – and he never missed. We never put the bar up to anybody but he had to have the bar up. It was a time when you couldn't get chocolates, they were terribly difficult to get. He'd come down and win all the chocolates, all the cigarettes and off he'd go. He was allowed 6 or 7 goes, I think; they were 7 [goes] for sixpence...I don't think he ever missed and he'd take away his 6 or 7 prizes.

In the 1920's, Daisy's brother Tom invested in fruit machines:

Later on Tom had fruit machines, the original ones. For some reason the Government of the time stopped it as a game of chance and not skill and they were stopped for a period.⁽⁵⁾ All these obsolete fruit machines were stored in the house in the loft. Down came a man who offered them a wonderful price for them and paid for them and never did collect the machines. They were sold and never collected. I think my brothers reopened them again later on. The top prize was three black bars [that could be exchanged] for twenty discs. You could put them in the machines again at the end of the game or you could change them for swag.

Bronze-coloured discs that were exchanged for prizes
©Cain family archive

Fred was Daisy's favourite brother and she was devastated when he died just 3 weeks after "giving her away" at her wedding to Ernest Bell in 1928. *See also pp. 33–34.* Fred was a very popular man as witnessed by this extract from his obituary in the *World's Fair*:

> When the fine four-horse hearse drove into the [show] ground, with a splendid team of jet black Belgian horses... the High Street was a packed mass of people lined up on either side of the street four and five deep, shepherded into position by the police on duty...all traffic came to a voluntary stand still...faces were at every window above the shop premises en route.

Daisy also referred to her brother Dave in her album, who sadly died in 1940, leaving a widow Ada and daughter Vera. *See also p.39.* Dave had acted as a driver driving 'to distant fairgrounds'. According to Daisy, he at one time opened a second fairground at the top end of the High Street that he named "Coney Island".

Here is how Dave's funeral was movingly described in the *World's Fair*:

> The setting for the memorial service...was very appropriate, for in the centre of the dodgem track on the fairground in High Street Deptford, stood the beautiful oak coffin on a bier, with the family and a large circle of friends standing around...The Rev. Dumphreys [gave his] address, including the following words: his object in life, in association with his family were to provide amusement, fun, competitions, all to try and make us happy, to give us a break from our sordid lives, and to try and get us to forget our cares and worries. *World's Fair*, 22nd June 1940.

Dave Cain in his First World War uniform in 1918
©Bell family archive

Daisy was very proud of her showman heritage and its links with circuses. In her album there is a photo of Ada Irvin, *née* Pinder, her friends Ada's grandmother, who had worked as a young woman as a bare back rider in her family circus 'Pinder's' and also in Sanger's circus. Ada's aunt, Florrie Irvin married Albert Hickey, who also worked for Sanger's Circus in 1901 and was renowned for bringing over from the United States the first "Unrideable Mule" circus act.

Ada Pinder ©Bell family archive

Florrie Irvin and her half brother Harry as children
©Bell family archive

Notes and references

(1) Ada Irvin was a great friend and distant cousin of Daisy Cain; they were born in the same year and were very close. Ada's father, Harry Irvin, worked in Cain's warehouse for many years. *See p.47 and above.* Ada later became godmother to Daisy's son Peter. She remained best friends with Daisy until her death in 1963; in her will she left her mink coat to Daisy and her grand piano to Peter!

(2) Zeppelins were a type of airship used by the German army to carry bombs during the First World War from May 1915 onwards. By January 1916 they had made twenty-one raids over London, dropped 1,900 bombs totalling over 32,000 kg, killed 277 and

wounded 645. Deptford would have been especially vulnerable due to their inaccuracy and also to its proximity to the Thames Docks, a favoured target. They were virtually unstoppable until 6 June 1916, when the British developed a rudimentary air defence system. *International Encyclopedia of the First World War, 1914–1918-online.*

(3) Rumours circulating in Deptford attributed this explosion to a Germany factory that was thought to have been sabotaged; in fact it was caused by an accident at a British munitions factory: 50 tons of TNT exploded killing 73 people and injuring many more. 19th January 1917, Silvertown, West Ham. *Daisy Bell unpublished recordings* and *Wikipedia.*

(4) A 'pullin ball' game was a kind of 'bagatelle': a sloping glass topped table with a chute at the side and a spring plunger that you pulled back. When it was let go it propelled a celluloid ball around the curved top of the board and it and subsequent balls would fall into numbered slots. The total of the numbers were added up to win a prize. *Kevin Scrivens, unpublished information.*

Memories of Dorothy Reeves, *née* Moore (1934–), daughter of Florence Cain, as shared with the author

©Bell family archive

Dorothy has strong memories of being part of the Cain Show Ground family in Deptford and her family heritage is very important to her. In a room in her old flat in Portsmouth she had murals of two galloping horses, one named Charles and one named Hannah, in honour of her grandparents, painted by her husband Malcolm. See cover designs.

Dorothy with her husband Malcolm in front of a mural evoking
fairground life painted by Malcolm ©Malcolm Reeves

Dorothy vividly remembered visiting 'the Ground' as a child, especially the big gates at the entrance and stalls, with their exciting goods on display, down one side of the entry. She especially remembered the rather oily smell, maybe from the Dodgems or perhaps from the nearby railway. Of the rides she most remembered the Gallopers and the Dodgems. She had vague memories of a Helter-Skelter at the back of the Ground in the part of the yard where she was not allowed to go. She thought that this may have been where people were living in their caravans.

©Malcolm Reeves

The Show Ground house seemed very big to a young child. The entrance for the family was through the backway with the scullery where Esther, the family servant, presided. Then into a large room with a fire on the right and windows on the left. To a child it seemed as though the whole room was filled by a very large table, covered by a chenille cloth, with many heavy dining chairs round the edge. In the window was a couch where Grandma, Hannah, would sit, elegant and very well dressed. On the far side was the door to a large cupboard under the stairs. The inside of the door had rows of keys and her uncles would come in to get a set, or would hang a set on the door. There was a door to the hall and stairs which led to Hannah's bedroom where, if she was resting, Dorothy could go and talk to her. Dorothy only rarely went into the other downstairs rooms and never went into any other room. Dorothy remembered her grandmother with great fondness:

She was a lovely, kind woman. When we were ready to leave, she always gave me some money to share with my brother Raymond. "Will you give him the heads or the tails", Grandma always joked.

Hannah Cain ©Bell family archive

Dorothy's mother, Florence, tended to be quite reclusive, rather strict and very pious. She preferred to visit the family when the Show Ground was closed. In her last years Florence sought to distance herself from the family. In spite of this, her sister Daisy organised meet ups of the three younger sisters and made sure they all kept in touch. In the end Florence stopped joining them. Florence's strong principles also stopped her attending the annual Masonic dinner dances. Dorothy remembered being told that her grandfather Charles Cain had been Grand Master of the Masonic Lodge. *See Chapter 2*. There is a set of silver teaspoons which Florence's granddaughter, Sarah, now has. They were given to Florence even though she did not attend the annual Masonic dinner dances where sets were given.

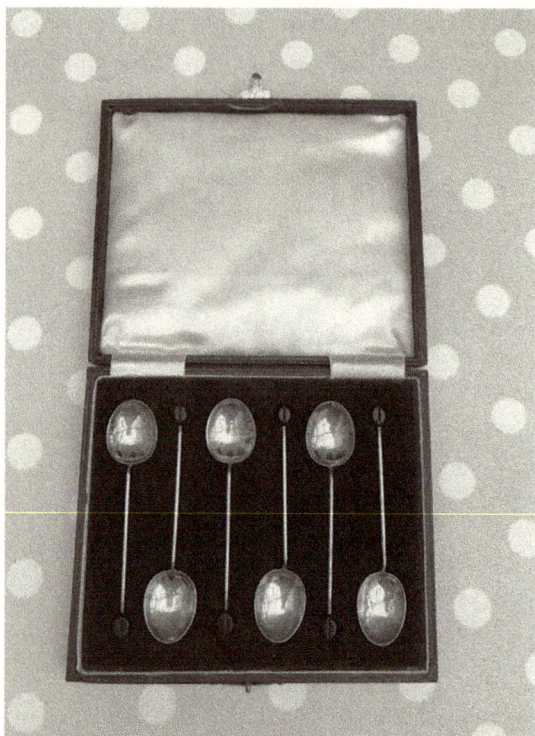

Present from a Masonic dinner dance ©Sarah Surr

Hannah died in 1946 when Dorothy was 12. When her grandmother was very ill, Dorothy had been given a message from one of her uncles to pass on to her mother that her grandmother had had a stroke. Dorothy had been too frightened of her mother's likely reaction to pass on the message, and then got into trouble when her mother found out that Hannah was so ill and she hadn't known that she needed to visit.

Dorothy had never known her grandfather Charles as he had died before she was born. However, she remembered a family story which illustrated how good a businessman he was. Early in his career in Aylesbury, he had apparently bought a litter of piglets from a farmer who was having trouble selling them and promptly sold them for double what he had paid. Grandma proudly had told Dorothy how Grandfather had thrown knives around her in his knife-throwing act.

Grandfather Charles Cain died a rich man; his will stated that he owned twenty-three houses. After Charles' death Hannah spent a lot of money on holiday cruises. Dorothy recalled how his daughters weren't allowed to inherit money directly and only received money from the houses in the form of rents, to prevent their husbands getting hold of the family fortune. This had been a bone of contention among his daughters. Dorothy recalled how her grandfather Charles didn't really value education because he had done well without it. This especially applied to his daughters. Dorothy knew that Florence and Daisy had won scholarships to Grammar School but had not been allowed to continue after the official leaving age of 14.

Dorothy remembered Esther, the much-loved family servant, taken in "as a waif" always working in the scullery. She remembered that Esther had a hair lip. On reading Grandfather Cain's will Esther found he had left her £100 in his will (£7,000 in today's money) on condition she was still in his employ at the time of his death.

Esther Sorrell, much loved family servant
"who brought us up" *Daisy Cain*
©Bell family archive

Dorothy remembered three of her uncles and their wives. Uncle Charlie's first wife, Edith Faulkner, who died from tuberculosis in 1943 was well dressed and wore beautiful hats. Florence told Dorothy of the family story of someone shouting out to Edith in her younger days: *"Fine feathers don't make fine birds, girl Faulkner"*.

Charlie Cain with his first wife Edith soon after their marriage in 1912
©Bell family archive

Dorothy also remembered her Uncle Dave who died many years after being injured in the First World War by mustard gas. When four or five years old, she visited his sickroom with her father and was aware of him struggling to breathe.

Dorothy talked about her aunt, the eldest daughter of Charles and Hannah, also called Hannah, who married the publican of the Green Man pub at Southend Pond, Catford. Apparently, she was deaf following a bout of scarlet fever in childhood. Dorothy remembers going with her mother to visit Hannah in hospital after she had fallen down the stairs of a tram. *See Ian Wake's memories.*

Another story Dorothy remembered from her mother is about of one of her uncles who as a child had a twitchy eye – this was probably Charlie. The doctor was invited to dinner with the family so he could check this out. The culprit did not twitch once while the doctor was there! Uncle Charlie was regarded as the comedian in the family.

Charlie Cain in a Scottish costume ©Cain family archive

Dorothy had a favourite aunt: lovely, bright, fantastic Aunty Daisy. She was small even by Cain standards but was a *"great ray of sunshine"*. Her needlework was wonderful; for

Dorothy's fifth birthday she made a pram set and outfits for two dolls. *"No one met Daisy without feeling cheered."* She and Florence continued to talk on the phone regularly. Dorothy would visit her mother some evenings after a long day at work only to find a call from Daisy in progress, with her mother attempting to finish the call. Peter, Daisy's son was the next youngest cousin in the Cain family, but Dorothy and Peter did not meet very often.

Florence, Dorothy's mother as a girl ©Bell family archive

When Dorothy was 8, she saw her cousins, Jack [John] and Barry Cain, sons of Uncle Charlie and Edith, in their service uniforms come to the Ground to say good bye before leaving to serve in the Second World War. Jack survived and received an honour[1] but Barry was killed in Norway when his plane was shot down. Some of the family have visited his grave. *See Chapters 2 and 5.*

Jack Cain

Barry Cain

Barry Cain's grave in Norway; *photograph taken by his brother Jack*
©Bell family archive

Dorothy's brother Raymond died in 2012 at the age of 89. Her other brother, John, died at the age of 3 before she was born.

Note

(1) Jack Cain was awarded the Distinguished Service Medal 'for courage, leadership and devotion to duty shown in Motor Torpedo Boat 733 and other light coastal craft in many successful engagements with the enemy in the English Channel.' *Daisy Bell's unpublished album.*

Memories of the author Angela Catherine Cain (1947–), granddaughter of Tom and Rose Cain, and daughter of Frank and Peggy Cain[1]

©Cain family archive

I remember visiting the Show Ground often during my early childhood until it closed when I was 13 in 1961.

I was 2½ when we moved out of Deptford to Beckenham, where my parents had bought a house opposite their parents Tom and Rose Cain. Tom was still running the Show Ground but commuting to Deptford every day.

There was a passageway leading to the main Show Ground from Deptford High Street where there were rather smelly market stalls all along the road. On the right there was an arcade area with lots of penny slot machines and fruit machines. They seemed very old to me. I especially liked the machines where you pressed a lever to activate balls into different slots. There were also round spinner games (shaped like a big Christmas cake) where you inserted a metal marble into a funnel at the top which you then spun to make the balls go where you wanted.

The fairground had a distinctive rather oily smell I remember. Once inside, there were big fairground rides. I remember Dodgems, a Skid and an Ark. I remember my grandfather Tom and grandmother Rose in the fairground house. I only remember the living room/ kitchen, with its big table covered in oilcloth. Rose used to make us sandwiches, always buttering the end of the loaf before cutting the bread, which always surprised me.

There was one particular visit when I was about 4 yrs old when we went to meet Frances Bailey for the first time – she had just become engaged to my Uncle Stanley Bill and was working on her family 'Ark' at the Show Ground. 'There she is, on the Ark" said my mother. I didn't understand she was in charge of the ride, so was looking for her on a motor bike, and just couldn't see her – I was very disappointed, though quite impressed by the ride I remember.

When I was older I remember going on the Ark lots of times and also a few times on the 'Skid' which I found really scary as the cars went backwards and forwards at great speed. The Dodgems too I found scary as they seemed hard to control. I have very vague memories of there being a shooting gallery and a 'Wall of Death' ride there too when I was very small, which seemed dark and smoky, not like this photograph.

Wall of death ride ©Irvin Leisure

Although I didn't know what it was until I read Stephen Smith's article in the 'Platform' magazine, I remembered this organ that was parked up on the Show Ground on the way to the Bingo Hall. It had a distinctive tinkly sound that I loved.

Close up of Cain's 87-key Gavioli organ © The Fairground Society

We also used to visit Stanley Bill and Frances Cain when their travelling fair visited Black Heath every Easter and summer bank holidays. My sister Jenny and I used to love this. Stanley Bill and Frances had two caravans: a large, luxurious upholstered 'wagon' which served as living area and bedrooms and a separate 'trailer' – a very large caravan used mainly as a kitchen and dining area. I remember how Frances supervised which rides were safe for us to go on and always made sure we had someone with us to look out for us – and she always made us ham rolls!

My Dad Frank used to go "Down the Grounds" and run the Bingo on Friday nights, which was in a separate building at the far end of the Show Ground. He always wore a tie and brylcreemed his hair, so running the Bingo would have been no exception.

Frank Cain ©Cain family archive

Frank Cain sitting by a joint in about 1934 with young cousins.
©Cain family archive

When we were old enough, we would go and meet my Dad at the end of the evening to give him a lift home. It was a completely different world to Beckenham. It must have been a very different world to that of my Dad's every day workplace: on weekdays he was a chartered accountant working in Harley Street. On Friday nights he became a showman. Jenny and I were allowed to play a couple of games of Bingo: when we won the game it was continued after so that people didn't think it unfair and complain. We loved winning a prize and there was a huge variety to choose from: glasses, jugs, cups and saucers, toys, thermos flasks etc. I remember there being a rather elderly lady called May who often won and played with four Bingo cards, "she always chose nylon stockings as prizes!". My Dad thought that she sold them "down the market", during the week, to pay for next week's Bingo games. On occasions, as I got older, I was also allowed to call a few numbers, which I loved doing. I remember the patter we used; every game started in the same way:

"Eyes down, lookin", for the first number in the box. It's Bingo, by jingo, the old-fashioned game played in the new-fashioned way . A line to win: up and down the card, across the card, or corner to corner.

Many of the numbers had different names that everyone would join in with chanting them. For example: "Cup of tea, number 3", "Knock at the door, number 4", "One fat lady, number 8". The games were often played very fast, so as to get as many games played as possible. Metal bottle tops were used to cover the numbers.

Bottle tops used to cover the Bingo numbers

When I read Stanley Bill's obituary in 2016, I learned that he too had run the Bingo at the Show Ground. Here is a photo of my cousin David Senior following in the family tradition as a young man.

David Cain Senior as a young man running the family Bingo on the fairground at Dover ©David Cain Senior

I remember going to the Show Ground on the last day after the fairground closed, and feeling very sad. The Ground was nearly empty and everything moveable was being burned on a huge bonfire. There was talk in the family about the Dodgems being sold

to America, There was also talk of the organ being sold. I don't know what happened to them. I remember fantasising about how I personally might keep them in store until I was older and run the family fair again.

My sister Jenny died in 2015 and sadly was not able to contribute to this book.

Note

(1)   Rose Cain 1890–1963.
      Frank Cain 1916–1986.
      Peggy Cain 1920–2011

Memories of Rosanne (1963–) and David Cain Senior (1956–) son and daughter of Stanley Bill and Frances Cain, *née* Bailey, and grandchildren of Tom and Rose Cain[1]

David Cain Senior carrying his sister Rosanne at
the family's travelling fair
©David Cain Senior

The Show Ground closed when David Senior was just five and before Rosanne was born. David Senior's only direct memory was going to the Show Ground to remove the safe after it closed down – which they still use in their business today. They are very proud of their Deptford Show Ground heritage and over the years many showmen they have talked to have linked the name 'Cain' back the Show Ground in

Deptford and to the buying of swag. Their cousin Frankie Bailey shared with them that he had gone to "the Ground" with their dad Stanley Bill to help out. For instance they had run the Bingo together. While clearing the Show Ground, Frankie's job had been to take some of the remaining swag to local shops to sell.

The family still have gold leaf and a transfer from the family logo they used on their lorries; David Senior remembered they were bought new from Fry's of Lewisham. David Senior and Rosanne had reminisced with Aunt Louise, their mother's sister-in-law, who remembered that after the Second World War the Bailey family had two rides at the Show Ground, an Ark and a Skid.

Bailey's Ark at Deal on 1 September 1959
©Jack Leeson/National Fairground Archive

Bailey's Skid ©Michael A. Smith

The family would travel by train from their winter quarters in Dartford to run the rides. It was their mother Frances' job to work on the Ark: "she didn't like the Skid", said Aunt Louise.

Frances had met her fiancé Stanley Bill at the Show Ground while working there. David Senior remembered a piece of Wedgewood china they had inherited from their grandad Tom that had come from the Show Ground house. Their dad had told them that when anyone went to buy swag they always bought back something for themself as well. *See over for examples.*

A table lamp from the Show
Ground ©Sarah Surr

A china horse from the Show
Ground, believed to be Wedgwood.
©David Cain Senior

Note

(1)   Stanley Bill Cain 1923–2016
       Frances Cain 1927–1987

Memories of Ian Wake (1972–), great great grandson of Charles and Hannah Cain

©Ian Wake

Charles Cain (1861–1935) was my great great grandfather. He married Hannah Knighton on 28 April 1884 and their eldest daughter, also called Hannah (1886–1952) was my great grandmother. She married my great grandfather, Alfred George Parrish who had my grandfather – Alfred Parrish (1911–1981) who married my grandmother – Olive Maud Troke (1912–2010) who had my mother – Carol Anne Parrish.

I do have some information about the Show Ground in terms of stories, largely from my late grandmother – Olive, with whom I was incredibly close. Olive also grew up in South London, but from a pretty poor background. Charles Cain and his wife Hannah Knighton were very wealthy. His probate shows a legacy that would be worth several million pounds in today's money. He made his wealth from both the Show Ground – hugely popular in an age free of television or anything digital, and also from a china and glass import business. He also owned several large town houses near Deptford High Street.

Olive Trope, Ian Wake's late grandmother ©Ian Wake gap

My grandmother told me stories of being taken to visit Charles Cain and his wife Hannah Knighton on Deptford High Street when she married my grandfather. She told me of an enormous house filled with fine furniture and servants and packed with fine glass and china, and being rather overwhelmed by it all, as it was so different to her own background. I remember her telling me that the Cain's would allow her to pick a piece of glassware or china ware every time she visited to take home as a gift. She also told me when she visited Charles Cain and Hannah Knighton's house as a young married woman, she was amazed that the servant would cook her anything she requested.

I also remember her telling me of the story when Hannah Knighton died in 1946 and the funeral. She spoke of the coffin being placed on a horse drawn by four fine horses and the entire streets of Deptford being lined by people who had come out to pay their respects. By all accounts, Charles Cain and Hannah Knighton were quite the local celebrities!

Ian Wake's great grandmother Hannah, Charles and Hannah's eldest daughter ©Ian Wake

Chapter Four

The people of Deptford remember

This chapter is drawn from memories shared by people who grew up in Deptford in the nineteen forties and fifties, mainly from the Facebook Group "I grew up in Deptford, SE8, London" and other on-line platforms. It has been a joy to hear everyone's stories; thanks to everyone for sharing them.

Many people still have very fond and vivid memories of the Show Ground, seeing it as an important part of their childhood and teenage years:

> *Bumper cars...penny a time...gambling machines...air rifle stall...and Frankie Laine records: magic for me at the time in the fifties.* John William Cripps

> *"It was there for years and pretty much taken for granted, I loved it."* Betty Morris.

> *"I loved the fairground. I was always down there as a kid."* Tessa Doreen Nuttman.

> *"Those were the days. They used to give free tickets to the girls to encourage the boys to go on the rides."* Annie Goodall.

And for Anne Hailstone, it was her very first visit, when she was just four years old, that stuck in her mind:

> *"I remember my first visit to the Show Ground. I was probably about 4 (in 1957). I was so excited to be allowed to go on the*

roundabout with all the different rides on it. I chose to go on the double decker bus with my 3 year old sister. Up the stairs I went in such a hurry, to get in the front seat, that I banged my head on the hot light bulb hanging down. I remember crying, but insisted on staying on the ride to the end. Still remember it like it was yesterday!"

Saturdays were big days at the Show Ground:

Lionel Baughen: *"As a kid, Saturdays was the day down there, good times: fun of the fair and Dodgems and penny machines."*

"My mum used to take us there on a Saturday night in the fifties and when we got older we used to go with friends. I loved it there." Barbara Phillips.

And for Joan Grigsby and Terry McCarthy it was Boxing Days that were special:

Terry McCarthy: *"I loved it. It was always open on Boxing Day."*

Joan Grigsby: *"We went there on Boxing Day. We spent money we got for Christmas. I went with my two sisters and little brother. We loved it: dodgems, machines, winning half pennies and pennies, coconut shy and darts in cards. It wasn't far from our house in Church Street. Lovely memories! You went through two big red gates in the High Street by Dr. Conway's surgery."*

Several people mentioned that members of their family had worked there. Rob Broad said that his mum used to work in the arcades. Linda Pampling shared how her grandad had worked there. Also, that she had been bitten by the guard dogs – an unfortunate memory shared with Linda O'Hara, who remembered her brother and friends being chased by the dogs.

Some people reported that the Show Ground was important to their families in earlier times:

> *"My mum remembers the Show Grounds, she was always hopping off school to go there and win a penny: 'Hopping the wag' ".* Robert Goshawk.

Rita Knight didn't remember going to the Show Ground herself, but knew that it was where her parents had first met in 1936–7, before they married in February, 1938.

Leslie Buckingham recalled how his grandfather, Bill Buckingham, used to fight in the boxing booth *"many, many years ago"* at the Show Ground:

> *"My grandfather...would have been a heavyweight as he was about 6 ft 3ins and about 17 stone. He was known as "Battling Bill Buckingham". He was born between 1896–1898 and in the later years the family lived in Church Street, Deptford. He died in 1973. He was, as I understand, a formidable street fighter. I suppose size, weight and strength had a lot to do with it."*

Bert Bowes remembered his father's stories about a bare knuckle boxing booth at the Show Ground, where you could *"try your luck"*. Jimmy White's nephew also shared:

> *"Jimmy White was a regular at the boxing booth [at the Show Ground] fighting at strawweight, a little heard of fighting weight nowadays. My uncles told me he was a devastating little boxer who went on to become Southern Area champion whilst serving in the Army."*

Some people knew the Cain family. Danny Durnford recalled being a friend of the Cain boys: *"we got in and stole the Spangles."* Billy Garrett remembered the owner:

> *"'A little man with a trilby hat', telling me off for climbing on a wall: I did not see the electric cable until my leg touched it. Last thing I remember was flying through the air, landing in the old garden grass with burns on my leg. Did not do it again!"*

And for Jean Dorton it was perhaps a guilty pleasure: *"I remember the Show Ground well. I was always warned not to go there!"*

The entrance stood out for some people. Ray Blake recalled *"There was a peanut stall at the entrance."* Anthony White mentioned the coloured lights as you entered the Show Ground: *"There used to be coloured light bulbs running around the metal hoops, all lit up of the nighttime, letting you know they were open."*

A punch ball near the entrance was a significant memory for both Anthony White and James Anthony Mcdaid:

Courtesy of James Anthony Mcdaid

"The first thing you'd see when you were going in was the punch ball. All the men would have a go to see who could get the highest score ...It was the first thing all the young lads saw and queuing to have a go." Anthony White.

"Another memory of the Showground was the punch ball/bag, similar to the one in the photo. Being too small at the time, I watched the older lads hit the ball as hard as they could. I think it cost around 1d a punch. Walking away after watching for around ten minutes, I thought how glad it was not my face being hit as, to a little boy, some of them hit the ball so hard." James Anthony McDaid.

The Dodgems or 'bumper cars' were a strong memory for some people.

"You walked down the alley with the hoops over and they were in front of you," said Trish Way Gage.

Dave Smeed recalled how he had been banned from them:

"Got banned from the 'bumper (no-bumping-allowed) cars' for dropping a few boxes of caps on the metal floor. Sounded like the O.K. Corral!"

And for ten year-old James Anthony McDaid:

"Being only a ten-year-old when the showground closed (1961), my memories are as seen by a little boy. My favourite was the dodgems/bumper cars. What stands out was the flashing from the top of the pole, which was at the back of the car, like a strobe light, especially at night. Plus, when one of the men jumped on the back to help with the steering, grabbing the wheel to help straighten up. Good memories for a young lad."

Dot Smith thought she remembered the name of the man who operated the Dodgems. *"If I remember rightly a fellow called Georgie Barefoot operated the Dodgems."*

A typical 1950s-style Dodgem track ©Pinterest

The music played was a very clear and important memory for some people:

"All the music was probably enjoyed by the Teddy Boys who 'hung out there'." said Tony Connell. John Carroll remembered they played rock n'roll. Sylvia Knox remembered *"Reet Petit"* *(Jackie Wilson, 1957)* and *"Bony Maronie"* *(Larry Williams, 1957)* and other people remembered Perry Como's *"Magic Moments"* *(1958)*. Guy Mitchell's *"She wears red feathers and a hula hula skirt"(1953)* and *"And Singing the Blues"* *(1956)* were remembered fondly by Dianne Pearson. *Cathy's Clown, (Everley Brothers, 1960)* was Diane Hardy's favourite: *"It was the first record I paid 3d to play on a jukebox in a cafe near Woolworth's!"*

Barbara Scott said she wasn't old enough to go to the Show Ground but remembered hearing *"O Carol"* by Neil Sedaka

(1959) when she went past on Saturday nights *"to get saveloys and pease pudding down the High Street."*

The penny arcade machines were some people's favourite:

Eileen Paget: *"I absolutely loved to put a penny in one of those machines. Such innocent times."* Pat Norman remembered there were the fruit machines as you walked in on the right. Dave Smeed reminisced that he had *"found a way of winning in the penny barrel machines!"*

Billy Garrett mentioned a rifle shooting game at metal ducks that he loved to play. Alan Spencer remembered that corks were used as targets. Pat Norman especially remembered the 'Wall of Death' with motor bikes; Anthony White remembered roller skating.

It's been harder to find memories of the Bingo: it would probably have been frequented by older family members. However, Billy Garrett thought he remembered playing Bingo in a bell tent in the left side corner next to the bumper cars, before it moved to its own building on the right. Barbara Phillips remembers her mum winning lots of prizes such as a lovely mirror, little cups and saucers and glasses. Christopher McCarthy recalled that players were seated in a circle facing inwards with the Bingo caller in the middle. He remembered that numbers were recorded on a board with slide windows.

Thanks for these lovely glimpses into times past: As Eileen Paget said: *"Such innocent times."*

Chapter 5

A historical perspective

"What would a foreigner find most typical of English pastimes in 1928?

Is it the racecourse, the boxing ring, the theatre, or the football field? No doubt these are all popular, but the visitor would miss the most typical and traditional of all English recreations if nobody introduced him to the Fairground...[where] we come into the closest touch with the life of our forefathers."

Sunday News, 24th October 1928.

London had a long history of travelling fairs, some by ancient charter such as Bartholomew Fair, or ancient custom such as Black Heath and Mitcham, going back to Saxon times:

The victorious Normans brought with them the concept of the fair as a major trading event, and used the establishment of such fairs for both political and economic purposes. *Frances Brown (a)*

Deptford also had its own 'charter fair' behind the Rifleman pub. During the 1820s 'Deptford Fair' took place on Trinity Monday *"with many drinking and dancing booths and Richardson's Theatre attending"* (*Stephen Smith*) and where, according to *Frances Brown* (a), the Duke of Wellington marched in procession with the children.

The 1861 Census showed a number of showmen present in Deptford on Census Day: the enumerator, a Mr. Beard, noted that there were a number of travellers and hawkers in Lower Street occupying ground with refreshment stalls, shows and amusements. On another site, Andrew Purchase's Waxworks Show was in Deptford at the same time:

The show had its own bandsmen who played on the front. Inside it featured a host of murderers' heads, representations of Daniel in the lion's den and the death of Napoleon Stephen Smith.

The latter part of the nineteenth century saw a huge increase in 'newer fairs' due to greater affluence and more leisure time following the 1871 Bank Holidays Act, and ever more sophisticated entertainments enabled by new technology.

The Showmen's Guild, and its precursor the Showmen and Van Dwellers Protection Association, played a large part in professionalising and raising the profile of showmen. As the Showmen's Guild still does today, they campaigned to protect the rights and traditions of their members, fighting against the Gaming Acts that discriminated against fairs – in particular the 1853 Betting Act and the 1909 Moveable Dwellings Bill. They successfully resisted plans to regulate the lives of travellers as had already been done to barge dwellers over issues of cleanliness, morality and children's education.

After five years of campaigning, the showmen were rewarded by the defeat of the [Moveable Dwellings Bill]. The struggle taught them lessons. They realised what could be achieved if they worked together against forces traditionally opposed to their interests. A new self-image emerged in the course of the conflict. They began to see themselves as respectable businessmen, amusement caterers, proprietors of machines, not on any account to be confused with gypsies, hawkers or pedlars. *Frances Brown (a)*

In 1898 when a private members' bill threatened the very existence of fairs, the Showmen's Guild employed someone to check all the relevant bills and a number were overturned. In 1902 the Guild successfully negotiated that any yard or plot of land that had been open for two years or more could be designated as an official fairground; from 1903 Guild members were given priority on pitches:

The new century [twentieth] is pregnant with great opportunities for all sorts and conditions of showmen... [it's] more and more necessary that bright and morally wholesome amusements shall be provided for busy workers of the Empire...[there are now] more fairs and shows than ever existed before.[1]

The fact that Biddall's were advertising from the Deptford Show Ground and elsewhere for 'coloured', then 'black or white' lion tamers in 1902 suggests that there was a pool of people from ethnic minority backgrounds to draw on within the showmen's world at this time. Show owners were always seeking novelty and innovation, and performers from different ethnic backgrounds would likely have been seen as 'exotic' and interesting and therefore valued. Boxers with a Black heritage were also working in London from the early nineteenth century, including Harry Sutton, corn porter and 'boxer' from Deptford and James Wharton, seaman and 'prize fighter'; Duse Moh'd Ali, born in Egypt is known to have worked in travelling theatres in London, which may have visited Deptford. *Black Londoners, UCL website*. Thomas Horne, Chaplain of the Showmen's Guild wrote in 1905 about racism in the industry and claimed there was "no colour line...the only test being ability." Professor Vanessa Toulmin comments that while this needs to be understood within the culture of the day towards anyone who was considered different, *'circus presented an opportunity and escape from prevailing attitudes of gender and racism.'* Vanessa Toulmin [2]

In 1906 the *Era* newspaper was highlighting the increasing professionalism of showmen:

> Years ago they were merely freak shows or some kind of catch-penny entertainment. Now better ideas prevail, more mechanism is used in the production of shows, and a great deal more money is expended by showmen in seeking to meet the public taste. Today many more thousands of pounds are laid out on a good travelling show...It has become an organised, legitimate and respectable industry. *Era*, 18 August 1906, Frances Brown (b).

What life would have been like for the Cain family as travelling showmen, before they settled in Deptford, we only get small glimpses. "Lord" George Sanger's vivid autobiography of his early life on the road with his family in the mid 19th century gives us some clues. Sanger painted a world of hugely resourceful, versatile and determined showmen. And yet it was a *very* hard life where certain incidents and anecdotes seem almost commonplace: cholera and smallpox; rivalries between showmen; clashes with the law; fights between gypsies and showmen; accidents; the need to travel together for protection from robbers; and hardship in the winter months. *"Lord" George Sanger.*[3]

By the time Charles Cain had the funds to buy the Deptford Show Ground in 1912 he was 51 and had served a long apprenticeship – over thirty years – as both a showman and a swag merchant. His daughters were 26, 18, 12 and 7 by this time and the eldest, Hannah, was already married.

His four sons were all in their 20s – all showmen with their own fairground speciality and all with a role in the swag business. It's not surprising that Charles Cain sought a higher standard of living, greater security and social status than had been possible when travelling. That the Cain's were attracted to Deptford made complete economic sense. With a high population, high employment and relative affluence, it was a perfect choice.

It was fortuitous timing for Charles Cain to have taken over the Show Ground in 1912: the introduction of steam power and then electricity enabled the mechanisation of fairgrounds, resulting in bigger and more sophisticated rides, such as the prestigious Gallopers by Savages that arrived on the Show Ground in 1916.

Mechanisation made the fairground appear modern and futuristic...[it] came at a most opportune time in its history...it revitalised the...fairs and created a hierarchy of businessmen on the fairgrounds.[4]

By the time Charles Cain acquired the Show Ground, Bioscope and Cinematograph shows were being superseded by permanent cinemas.[5] Variety shows, striptease shows and wild west shows; freak and curiosity shows and boxing booths were holding their ground for the time being. Electric light made for a brighter and safer fair, superseding candles, flares, naptha, oil lamps and then gas lights.

The two World Wars were a major challenge to showmen generally and during the First World War especially, many travelling fairs were forced to close, and all fairs closed from September 1916 for a time. On the other hand, in wartime fairs were seen as much needed relaxation for the workers:

Amusement and recreation for the workers were [considered] a national necessity...all classes of entertainers were a national necessity...all classes of entertainers were helping to win the war by maintaining the morale and sanity of both toilers and fighters.[6]

And in the Second World War:

When a state of hostilities was declared in September 1939 the [Showmen's] Guild immediately contacted the government to lobby for the continuation of travelling fairs. Overall, fairgrounds were allowed to continue under blackout conditions.[7]

Blackout rules restricted activities in both World Wars. For example, during the First World War, Government guidelines restricted the quality of light from fairs:

...for the period from one hour after sunset till one hour before sunrise...so shade or reduce the lights that no more than a dull subdued light was visible from any direction outside. *Frances Brown (b)*

Although there is no direct record from Deptford itself, fear of zeppelins caused police to ban naptha flares and large electric lamps at Mitcham Fair during the First World War. Also, twenty-six horses were requisitioned from Mitcham Fair in 1914 and later on traction engines were also requisitioned. This resulted in some showmen negotiating a contract with the War Office to drive their own traction engines. *Frances Brown (a)* Hannah Cain's half brother, William Irvin, was perhaps one of these traction engine drivers. He sadly died when some logs fell on him when moving them with his traction engine during War Service.[8]

'Merry-Go-Round' by Mark Gertler, a stylised view of Hampstead Heath Fair painted in 1916 – believed to be an expression of the horror of war; *Charles Cain was reportedly very unhappy about his sons going to war* ©Tate

The Showmen's Guild actively supported the war effort in each World War and encouraged showmen to 'send their sons to war and their daughters to work in munitions'; it also donated eight ambulances to the Red Cross 'For King and country' in the First World War and a Spitfire named 'The Fun of the Fair' in the Second World War.[9]

Dorothy Moore, Florence Cain's daughter, remembers the large crowds which surged onto the Show Ground most evenings throughout the Second World War: "*...eager to enjoy themselves and for a few hours to forget the horror around them of the bombing and destruction.*"

Tom Cain's wife, Rose, wrote to her daughter-in-law (my mother Peggy), saying how overwhelmingly busy the Show Ground was on Boxing Day 1944 and in the next paragraph calmly explaining how a bomb had fallen on a street near where they lived:

Had a nasty Rocket this week smashed houses...in Adolphus Street and Payne Street and plenty of damage to our own house [in Octavius Street], so far 18 deaths and plenty of injured. We had doors off. The back room wall fell down and plenty of minor damage, but we are still here to tell the tale, very tired as you can guess after all the clearing up, dirt, dust, plaster bricks, soot everywhere but we are still smiling.[10]

The two World Wars were a time of personal tragedy for the Cain family. *See Chapters 2 and 3.* They also seem to have been a time of growth and expansion of the Show Ground: the Gallopers arrived part way through the First World War and the Dodgems arrived in 1939. *See Chapter 2.* In the First World War, not all Charles' sons went to war. Tom avoided call-up due to flat feet, a reason for refusal due to the need to be able to march long distances; Fred's long illness also would have prevented him going to war.

Showmen's Guild war memorial at the National Memorial Arboretum, Staffordshire; *see Barry Cain's commemoration in the London Section part of the memorial.* ©Cain family archive

Women have always played a major role on fairgrounds, witness Hannah Cain's role working on the family's Gallopers and early side shows and her important organising role in billing customers and ensuring swag was sent to the right station. Cain's Amusements today relies heavily on the administrative skills and talent of Rosanne Cain, who serves as its Financial Director, and her sister, Francesca, who helped manage the Herne Bay arcade for many years; she was very much the heart and soul of their entire business until her recent retirement for health reasons. Tracy, wife of David Cain Senior, has also long been involved in the business as a manager of the Herne Bay arcade.

Rosanne, Tracy and Francesa Cain (l to r) ©David Cain Senior

In 1916 the following editorial appeared in the *World's Fair*:

> In showland, women have always worked and worked hard. We have seen our women at the head of circuses, menageries, roundabouts and many other amusement concerns, and in fully ninety per cent of our people, it is the women who look after the exchequer.[11]

There are numerous examples of women being in charge of fairs, sometimes on the death of a spouse, with a family to feed; indeed, it was Mrs. Weatherhead who played a prominent role in her family business and went on to sell the Show Ground to Cain's. In both wars, it was often the women and "invalids" who took over the running of the fairs. We know that Charles Cain had an ambivalent view of women and their roles. While the girls of the family were expected "to help out" and pull their weight on the rides and stalls, they don't seem to have had any major planning or innovative roles in the family business. Charles was more protective of them than anything, while ensuring their welfare in a way that he felt would not harm the family. *See Chapter 3.*

We know from Dorothy Moore's recollections, that Charles Cain did not want his daughters to attend school beyond the compulsory school leaving age, because *he* had managed without education.[12] His oldest children, too, may have missed out on a regular formal education because they would probably have been travelling in the summer. However, Dave Cain's obituary mentions him having two local Oxford scholarships with honours - so he, at least, must have thrived at school.

Reaching back into the nineteenth century, all Cain birth and marriage certificates are signed with a cross, so being literate wasn't necessary to being a successful showman.

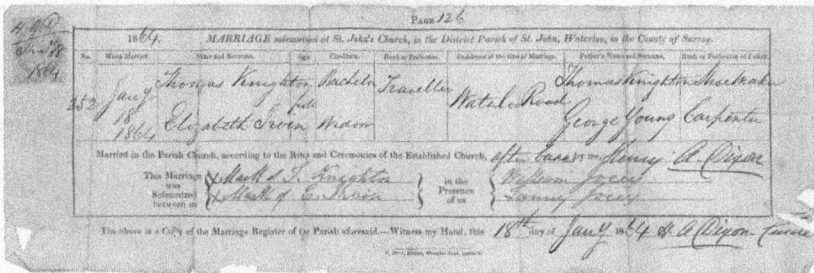

Marriage certificate of Thomas Knighton, Traveller, to Elizabeth Irvin, parents of Hannah Cain, signed with a X, 1864 ©Cain family archive

Tom and Charlie made sure their eldest sons were well educated, and sent them to St. Olave's Grammar School, which would have been fee paying at that time.[13] This perhaps explains why there was no one wanting to inherit the Show Ground: Jack Cain, son of Charlie went to Oxford University where in 1934 he was awarded an Open Exhibition in modern history and in 1937 a B.A. Honours, Oxford. Frank Cain, son of Tom, became a chartered accountant based in

Harley Street – while still running the Bingo on the Show Ground at weekends.

I think Charles and Hannah Cain would have been secretly proud (if not puzzled by) the successes of their descendants, among whom are graduate musicians, a children's social worker, a leading social policy local government officer and computer specialists. I think they would have reserved their greatest pride for their grandson, Stanley Bill, and his family, who went on to travel in the family showman tradition before settling down, as they themselves had chosen to do, as prestigious entrepreneurs and showmen on the south coast — while continuing to support the travelling members of their mother's family. In turn, Charles' father, Grandad David (who died in 1896 and didn't live to see his son's success), would no doubt have been very proud that Charles had gone from being a 'hawker and traveller' with his own horse and cart in 1891 to a showman of status and highly successful businessman, with a whole fleet of lorries, by the time of his death in 1935. I think that Hannah Cain – who after all had dreams of becoming a teacher – would also have been delighted and proud to see Tidemill Academy, Deptford Lounge and other community buildings on the site of the Show Ground fifty years after its closure.

It doesn't matter if your horse is going up or going down

Just so long as it keeps going around

Courtesy of George Irvin © Irvin Leisure.

Notes and references

(1) 1904 Report of the Showmen's Guild of Great Britain, National Fairground and Circus Archive.

(2) Toulmin, Vanessa, *Circus Show of Shows, What is Circus today? Explorations through 250 years of British Circus,* Circus250, University of Sheffield, 2018.

(3) Seventy Years a Showman by "Lord" George Sanger, George Cruikshank, Mathew Crampton and Kenneth Grahame, Muddler Book, 2018.

(4) Showmen's Guild of Great Britain, NFCA Archive.

(5) By 1912 there were around 6000 permanent cinemas in the country. Their flamboyant architectural design was thought to have been influenced by their fairground origins: 'a gaudy show front attached to a shed like auditorium'. *Richard Gray.* Cited by Kevin Scrivens and Stephen Smith in The Travelling Cinematograph Show, New Era Publications, 1999.

(6) NFCA Archive Research Article: *The First World War.* In September 1916 the Ministry of Munitions published an order to close all fairs for a time under the Defence of the Realm Act.

(7) NFCA Archive Research Article: *The Second World War.*

(8) www.irvinleisure.co.uk.

(9) The Spitfire was an F. Mark One built as a Mark VB type 331 built in 1941 and allocated to the 306 Polish Squadron; in 1942 it became part of the 315 Squadron. Showmen's Guild members had raised £5000 in four months to pay for it. *Information boards* at the National Memorial Arboretum, Staffs and NFCA research article: *The First and Second World War* and *The Showmen's Guild Role During the Wars.*

(10) Rockets or V2s, as they were known, were terrifying for the people of London. According to Dorothy Reeves, "*they just dropped out of the sky with no warning noise*". The Nazis targeted London and Antwerp from September 1944 with these long range weapons. They used liquid repellent and caused extensive damage and loss of life. www. worldwar2facts.org.

(11) *"There's no Women like Showwomen"* Dr. Vanessa Toulmin, National Fairground Archive, World's Fair June 27 – July 3 1997.

(12) The school leaving age was 12 in 1911 and raised to 14 in 1918.

(13) Charlie and Tom's younger sons' education was disrupted by the Second World War; Charlie's son Barry signed up at 17, pretending he was 18 and was killed in 1942; Tom's younger son Stanley Bill was at first evacuated to Torquay and then went on to serve as an engineer in the Royal Navy.

Glossary

Ark

Originally called a 'Noah's Ark', a fast fairground ride with motor bikes, animals or chariots that go both up and down (simulating a hill) and round and round.

Bingo

A game of chance in which people are given cards and cover each number on their cards as it is called, with the person who is first to cover a whole line of numbers being the winner.

Bioscope

An early film projector which enabled a sequence of images to be viewed and gave its name to a fairground show.

Cinematograph

An early moving film projector which gave its name to a fairground show.

Confetti

Small pieces of coloured paper that traditionally were thrown at special times of celebration including on the fairground.

Dodgems or 'bumper' cars

Fairground ride with small electrically powered cars where there are other cars to be dodged (or bumped into).

Gallopers

A roundabout, or carousel, with galloping horses, or other animals, that go up and down and round and round.

Helter Skelter

Shaped like a light house, it has an external slide in a spiral.

Joint

A stall or side show.

Menagerie

A nineteenth century travelling zoo that towards the end of the century became incorporated into Cinematographic shows and circus acts.

Naptha

A flammable hydrocarbon mixture used to fuel a lamp.

Riding master

Owner of rides who sub-lets ground to other showmen.

Skid

Fast fairground ride with spinning cars that go round and round and also spin on their axis; sometimes also known as a 'Waltzer'.

Swag

Fairground prizes.

Tilt

A canvas roof over a ride or side show.

Tober

A fairground.

Wall of Death

Fairground show that appears to defy gravity with motor cycles that seem to be ridden vertically around a wooden structure.

Acknowledgements

Huge thanks are due to members of the Cain family for providing information and photographs for this history of the Deptford Show Ground, in particular to Harley Bell, David and Rosanne Cain, Dorothy Reeves and Ian Wake, whose support and readiness to answer my endless questions was unwavering, no matter how busy they were. Thanks too to Malcolm Reeves for permission to use photographs of his beautiful fairground murals.

I am enormously grateful to Fairground Historians Frances Brown, Kevin Scrivens and Stephen Smith for their readiness to share their knowledge, photographs and answer my questions.

I wish to thank all the "Deptfordians" who provided the information for Chapter 4 and whose contributions inspired me to continue with this book when it seemed too daunting a task and to James Anthony Mcdaid, Deptford Historian, and Marion Drake, Headteacher of Tidemill Academy for their support and interest.

My grateful thanks and great respect go to Tim Ayres Jonathan Hyams, Jo Metcalfe, and Judy Tweddle for their advice, proofreading and editing skills and to Scott Turner for photo editing. And thanks too to Tanis Eve and her colleagues of Grosvenor House Publishing who so capably steered me towards "the finished book" with clarity and ease.

Thanks also to Matthew Neil of the NFCA library at Sheffield University, to the Showmen's Guild of Great Britain for permission to access their Archive, and to George Irvin of Irvin Leisure and to the many other people and organisations who contributed to this book in different ways. Finally, I am delighted to acknowledge the support of my husband, Julian Falk, whose readiness to read texts and manage computer glitches was a godsend.

Bibliography

Black Londoners, 1800–1900, University College London website. https://www.ucl.ac.uk/equiano-centre/projects/black-londoners-1800-1900.

Bell, Daisy. Unpublished album gifted to her grandsons Harley and Bruce Bell in 1977 and recordings made by Harley Bell with Daisy and her husband Peter in 1986.

Brown, Frances, Fairfield Folk, A history of the British Fairground and its People, Ronda Books, 1985 (a).

Brown, Frances, Fairground Strollers and Showfolk, Ronda Books, 2001. (b).

Booth, William, social reformer, cited by Wikipedia.

Downs, Carolyn. A History of Bingo in the UK, www.PlayingBingo.co.uk.

Fleming, Denis, The Manchester Fighters, Neil Richardson, Manchester,1986.

Green, Jeffrey. Black Edwardians, Black People in Britain 1901–1914, Frank Cass, 1998.

Golesworthy, Maurice, The Encyclopaedia of Boxing, Robert Hale, London, 1960.

Grahame, Kenneth, "*Introduction*" to Seventy Years a Showman by "Lord" George Sanger.

International Encyclopedia of the First World War. 1914-1918-online.

Irvin Leisure website, www.irvinleisure.co.uk "Irvin history".

Masonic Philosophical Society, www.philosophicalsociety.org.

National Fairground and Circus Archive research articles:

Bioscope Presenters: Alf Ball
The Fairground Bioscope Shows
Fairground Shows – A history from the Nineteenth Century
Few Punches More – The Fairground Boxing Shows
The First World War
History of the Fairground
History of the Showmen's Guild of Great Britain
Lighting on the Fairground
Mitcham Fair
There's no Women like Showwomen
The Second World War
The Showmen"s Guild Role During the Wars
Showmanship
Showmanship, Magic and Illusion
Showmanship and the Fairground Show
Showmen Families
The Fairground Enthusiast Movement in the UK
The Showmen's Guild of Great Britain Collection
The Showmen's Guild Role During the Wars

Sanger, "Lord" George, Seventy Years a Showman by "Lord" George Sanger, George Cruikshank, Mathew Crampton and Kenneth Grahame, Muddler Books.

Scrivens, Kevin and Smith, Stephen, The Travelling Cinematograph Show, New Era Publications, 1999.

Showmen's Guild of Great Britain, 1904, Annual Reports of 1904, 1907 and 1920, NFCA Archive.

Smith, Stephen, "*The Lost History of our Streets Deptford High Street*" in The Fairground Society magazine 'Platform', November, 2012.

Toulmin, Vanessa, *Circus Show of Shows, What is Circus today? Explorations through 250 years of British Circus*, Circus250, University of Sheffield, 2018.

Toulmin, Vanessa, National Fairground and Circus Archive "*There's no Women like Showwomen*", National Fairground Archive, World's Fair, June 27–July 3 1997.

White, Jerry, Zeppelin Nights in London in the First World War, Vintage Books.

www.worldwar2facts.org.

About the author

Angela
Catherine Cain

This is my first book, simmering away in me since 2012 when I watched a BBC programme about the history of Deptford High Street that made no mention of the Show Ground. Later, reading an article about it in The Fairground Society's magazine, '*Platform*', I realised there was a much bigger story to tell and that I wanted to tell it. Lockdown finally gave me the time and space to complete it. And by now, the need to make contact with Deptford people who might remember the Show Ground from the 1940s and 1950s was becoming urgent.

It's altogether been a hugely rewarding experience: connecting with fellow 'Deptfordians' through Facebook and learning about Deptford history through their memories; learning from Fairground Historians, who have been so very generous with their time and knowledge; and making links with family members who previously had just been names on a family tree.

Writing this book has been such a joy that I am already planning other books: a simpler book about the Show Ground for the children of Deptford and a book about Deptford High Street from before the First World War.